RELIGION
AND
THE WORLD ORDER

RELIGION AND CIVILIZATION SERIES

GROUP RELATIONS AND GROUP ANTAGONISMS
R. M. MacIver, *Editor*

RELIGION AND THE WORLD ORDER
F. Ernest Johnson, *Editor*

FORTHCOMING VOLUMES

CIVILIZATION AND GROUP RELATIONSHIPS
R. M. MacIver, *Editor*

INTELLECTUAL AND CULTURAL FOUNDATIONS OF WORLD ORDER
F. Ernest Johnson, *Editor*

RELIGION AND CIVILIZATION SERIES

RELIGION
AND
THE WORLD ORDER

A series of addresses and discussions

EDITED BY

F. Ernest Johnson

Professor of Education, Teachers College

Published by

INSTITUTE FOR RELIGIOUS STUDIES

Distributed by

HARPER & BROTHERS

NEW YORK AND LONDON

FOREWORD

The Institute for Religious Studies was established at the Jewish Theological Seminary of America by means of a gift from Lucius N. Littauer, Esq. Its purpose is to enable ministers of all faiths to study under the guidance of scholars in various fields, representing different religious groups.

The present volume contains a series of lectures under the general title "Religion and the World Order" given during the academic year 1942–1943. That the lectures vary widely in the degree to which they may be called religious in a technical sense will be at once obvious. By some readers this may be taken as an indication of a dilution of religious interest. But others will see in it a wholesome indication of the increasingly wide range of contemporary religious concern.

The reader will discover at once that the lectures vary considerably in form. This is due chiefly to the fact that some were submitted in manuscript, while others were taken down by stenotype as delivered. The undersigned, who acted as moderator of the course, has had the assistance of the lecturers in editing the manuscripts for publication.

THE EDITOR

August, 1943.

CONTENTS

Foreword vii

I. Contemporary Secularism as an Impediment to Religious Effort — *F. Ernest Johnson* 3

II. Trends in Religious Thought that Affect Social Outlook — *Paul J. Tillich* 17

III. Religious Liberty in the Postwar World — *Luther A. Weigle* 29

IV. Religion and Democracy — *Francis J. McConnell* 39

V. A Survey of Proposals for Postwar Reconstruction — *Henry P. Van Dusen* 53

VI. A Survey of Proposals for Postwar Reconstruction — *John LaFarge, S.J.* 67

VII. A Survey of Proposals for Postwar Reconstruction — *Ben Zion Bokser* 77

VIII. The Political Basis of Reconstruction — *Robert M. MacIver* 93

IX. The Economic Basis of Reconstruction — *Raymond Leslie Buell* 101

X. The Cultural Basis of Reconstruction — *Lawrence K. Frank* 113

XI. Education in the Postwar World — *George S. Counts* 131

XII. Reconstruction in International Law — *Clyde Eagleton* 139

XIII. Labor in the Postwar World — *John A. Fitch* 153

XIV. The Emerging Role of Government — *Edmund de S. Brunner* 167

XV. Opinion Making in the Postwar World — *Clyde R. Miller* 179

XVI. Lessons from the League — *Felix Morley* 195

XVII. Summary — *F. Ernest Johnson* 207

Index 217

CONTEMPORARY SECULARISM AS AN IMPEDIMENT TO RELIGIOUS EFFORT

By

F. ERNEST JOHNSON, D.D.

Professor of Education, Teachers College, Columbia University; Executive Secretary, Department of Research and Education, Federal Council of the Churches of Christ in America.

If an ancient Hebrew, Greek or Roman could return to earth and be set down in our midst today he would be quite bewildered by the subject of this lecture. Hardly less amazed would be a mediaeval European Christian. It would probably be very difficult to render the word "secular" in the language used by any one of them, for the concept would be alien to his mind. That word, in the context of this discussion, denotes something that is outside the realm of religious sanctions. To be sure, there have probably been unbelievers and heretics in every age, but in earlier times the man who rejected the gods of his people recognized himself as off the cultural reservation. In contrast to him, his modern irreligious brother is able to claim full membership in his community and partnership in its common life. Even the most religious of us would not question the good citizenship of a person who elects to stand outside the religious tradition of the Western world. Not only so, but the average religious person considers the greater part of his activities as outside the sphere of religious sanction. If one questions this statement let him consider the common demand that the Christian minister keep out of politics and business and "stick to the gospel." The idea, so familiar in the Middle Ages, that religion should furnish ethical standards for the governance of business and trade has little place in contemporary thought. Rather, the every day life of men is regarded as autonomous, without reference to any central body of ethical beliefs or spiritual aspirations. The slogan "Business is business" has become in a peculiar way characteristic of our age.

To designate this quality of the modern era I employ the word "secularism." It is not to be confused with the principle of the separation of church and state. Freedom of the state from church control and of the church from state control is required by the religiously heterogeneous nature of our population. And even if all citizens belonged to one church it would not follow that the boundary between the political and the ecclesiastical should become blurred. What is implied by secularism is that man's religious life is conceived as an inner and private affair, having no necessary relevance to his business or political activities and incapable of furnishing him with sanctions to guide his organized social relationships. Only exceptionally do we see a lay religious group seriously inquiring into the relevance of its religious faith to the conduct of business, industry or profession in which its members are engaged.

It is against this secularist mood and practice that the "social gospel" movement in the Protestant churches has been directed. It accounts for the formulation of "social creeds." A similar concern has prompted vigorous pronouncements by Catholic and Jewish bodies, of which there have been many in recent years. Some headway has been made in this effort to apply religious sanctions to the structure of modern society, against the secularist demand that the churches and synagogues leave business, industry and politics out of their sphere of attention and activity. The impact of the new prophetic religious testimony upon public and private ethical assumptions and practices is not negligible, but the fact remains that the social deliverances of the churches are largely of clerical rather than lay inspiration, and no broad sanction from the laity can be claimed for them. The great mass of activities that have to do with livelihood and the exercise of power remains subject to the operation of mechanisms of the market and and of practical politics, which acknowledge little obligation to the prophetic spirit of Judaism and Christianity.

It would completely misrepresent the situation to say that all who take the secularist position are supporters of the present secular order. Indeed some of the most uncompromising critics of contemporary industrial society are people who belong to no religious community and who make no more than vague pretensions to religious faith. Some of them, driven by their moral convictions, have given more ardent support to the social programs of the churches than has come from their most influential members. This anomaly deserves the most thoughtful scrutiny. On the one hand it indicates how in a secular age the church itself becomes secularized, forsaking its own tradition and conforming to the ethics of the market-place. On the other hand it indicates that many of those who have for intellectual or other reasons divorced themselves from all religious observances continue nonetheless to stand within the ethical tradition that takes its character from the Jewish and Christian faiths. Some among them are so disaffected with institutional religion that they hope to see the ethical core of the great religions embodied in the secular structure itself, leaving institutional religion behind as outmoded and unneeded. I think this hope is unrealistic in the extreme for reasons that will appear presently. But it would be folly for religious leaders who deplore the secularization of life and of the church itself to blind themselves to the significance of a vigorous social ethic that finds expression outside religious circles. The voices crying in the wilderness are not all within the ranks of organized religion.

The crucial question here is the nature of religion as a phase of the culture. In modern times the social role of religion has become so restricted that, as we have noted, it is commonly regarded as an individual concern, a body of private beliefs and attitudes that each person develops for himself much as he arrives at his political affiliations and his vocational choice. But this falsifies the nature of religion as history discloses it. From time immemorial religion has been a social phenomenon—an affair not of private but of communal concern. It has centered in a worshiping community and in essence it has always been group celebration of the highest values of the common life. Religion is primarily a corporate experience.

It is participation in a common spiritual heritage. Apart from such institutional expression it becomes a pale shadow of itself. To resolve religion into a set of private beliefs and attitudes is to destroy its essence. As well might we seek to cultivate familial attitudes and loyalties without the family, or patriotism without a country.

The effort to divorce the "religious" from "religion" which Mr. Dewey in some of his writing seems to advocate, is in reality an effort to end religion as a definite form of corporate experience. It is, to be sure, theoretically possible that religion in the future will be diffused over the whole institutional life of man and that he will no longer build churches, no longer maintain shrines. A perfectionist view of society may disclose a sunny future in which man's life will be so wholly sanctified that he will no longer need a sanctuary or symbols of the Highest before which to bow in company with his fellows. But such an assumption runs wholly counter, I think, to the record of history. To be sure, one can hardly fail to be impressed by the declaration of the saintly Brother Lawrence that he was as much in the divine presence when about his menial tasks in the monastery kitchen as when at the Blessed Sacrament. But Brother Lawrence was spared by his vocation from close contact with the world of affairs. He had, so to speak, specialized in sainthood and his whole life had become a prayer. As for those secular-minded persons of high character and social outlook to whom I have referred as putting to shame many who make high religious profession, yet who feel no need to worship—what shall be said of them? It is at least possible that many of them are living on spiritual capital accumulated by the religious communities in which they were reared and but dimly sense their indebtedness to a common religious tradition. However that may be, I venture to say that the masses of men will continue to feel the need for the institutions of corporate worship, however much their symbols and the intellectual formulations of their faith may change.

At any rate I should like to see the focus of discussion concerning the role of religion in life shifted from the private beliefs of individuals to the religious fellowship, the community of spiritual aspiration. The continuity of religious experience is found for the majority of us not in creeds, which continually undergo revision, but in the life of the worshiping community. Corporate worship, group celebration of the highest values, is the thing that unites all our several faiths.

If I am not mistaken, religious liberals, because of their tendency to over-intellectualize and over-individualize religious experience, miss the significance of the breakdown of the "mediaeval synthesis" and the consequent secularization of modern life. They see the incompatibility between the mediaeval world outlook and that of modern science, and they see in the passing of a rigid ecclesiastical control over life nothing to lament. What they do not see is that the fracturing of the spiritual community meant the loss of inclusive and unifying moral sanctions over the whole of man's activities. As a Protestant, I share the conviction of those who see authentic values in the Reformation, but I think all of us who stand in that tradition should see that a concomitant of the fragmentizing of Christendom was the divorcement of large areas of life from effective religious and moral sanctions—in other words, the rise of secularism. When the economic life of the Western world acquired a moral autonomy of its own the way was open to all the ills of unrestrained *laissez faire*. With the decline of the spiritual authority of the church in political affairs, however badly that authority may have been exercised, the way was open to the rise of nationalism as a false and pernicious religion. Can it be coincidence that the divorce of faith and reason, the dualistic conception of human nature and the rise of mechanistic natural science and psychology date from the time when the spiritual unity of the Western world was dissolving away? I would go even further and suggest that the triumph of nominalism in modern philosophy, with its restriction of reality to particular objects of sense, displacing the older realism with its insistence on the reality of universals, has played havoc with human society by sacrificing the philosophic basis of community.

Let us now consider in more detail the impact of a secular order of life on the church. Theologians make use of two concepts to characterize the inner corporate life of the Christian church and its effective social outreach. The compact, disciplined society which the word church ideally denotes is called the *Corpus Christi.* The community outside which accepts the teachings of the church and acknowledges their relevance to the common life, is referred to as the *Corpus Christianum.* The latter is an approximation to a "Christian society." Mediaeval Europe wore that aspect. No matter how remote men's daily living might be from the ideals they held, they acknowledged the authority of a common moral law and their responsibility to obey it. They dwelt under an inclusive spiritual sanction which the church symbolized though they could not qualify as faithful members of the *Corpus Christi.* The very structure of society derived its validity from this spiritual sanction.

Now it is this conception, stripped of all elements of ecclesiastical control over temporal affairs, that the social gospel movement has sought to clothe with life. Its aim is broadly ethical, and since the Christian social ethic derives specific content from the Old Testament prophets this social movement is within the Judaic-Christian tradition. It is an impressive fact that the social pronouncements of Catholic, Protestant and Jewish bodies are very nearly identical in purpose and tone. But because the Jewish community embraces so small a part of the population the Christian churches plainly have the major responsibility for winning acceptance of these ethical principles on the part of society as a whole. The effort to achieve this result in the modern world has been but slightly effective. The churches have gained no strong grip on the public conscience. Rather they have themselves become progressively secularized.

Let it be remembered that Christianity began as a Jewish sect and that even when it embraced Hellenic elements it remained for several centuries sectarian in the sense that it stood "against the world." The early church felt itself to be living in an alien environment, with which it had little in common. The *Corpus Christi* was powerless to create a *Corpus Christianum.* But as it gained influence it brought within its membership persons of wealth and standing, and, as we all know, was able to make Christianity the acknowledged religion of the Roman Empire. The church lost much of its inner purity in this process but the historic Christian movement could not have come about without this process of accommodation—except by the miracle of converting a vast population to the life of sainthood. At the apex of its power in the Middle Ages the church, whatever its failings, did have a grip on the conscience of the world in which it flourished. The spiritual and the secular, the temporal and the spiritual, were bound together by a common faith and a common world outlook. The Christian "sect," to employ a frequent usage, had become "church." Or, to express it otherwise, the church against the world had become the church astride the world.

Now the merit of the mediaeval regime is of course a highly controversial question. For many reasons most of us—Catholics as well as Protestants and Jews—would probably not wish to return to it. But my contention is that we are not entitled to turn our backs on the Middle Ages until we have learned to appreciate the value of a unified world-view and a common ethic and to assess soberly our loss in that the modern world has no cement to bind together personal morals and the morals of political and economic life. It is the function of religion to furnish that unifying force. And it is the very nature of secularism, in the strict sense of the word, to prevent that function from being performed.

For, as we have noted, the relationship between the church and the world is a two-way relationship. The more inclusive the church becomes the more it incorporates the world within itself. If society, in its structure, and particularly in its educational system, incorporates a body of convictions consistent with a historic religious tradition, organized religion becomes a steady disciplinary force operating to unify practice and theory, profession and life. But when the secular order denies the relevance of religious teaching to its own structure, a permanent dualism is established with resultant moral frustration. This is what we witness today. Our fathers were doubtless as great sinners as we are, but they at least had a moral compass to guide them. It has been said that the Puritan's religion did not keep him from sinning but it did keep him from enjoying it. That remark is something more than merely humorous. The conscious violation of a principle is less than deeply tragic if the person concerned has no doubt about his real status. But when vices are practiced in the name of virtue—as is so widely true of corporate competitive living today—the situation is tragic indeed, for the moral compass has been lost.

It must be noted that the mediaeval synthesis lost its grip on the Western world gradually, not by a sudden transformation of thought. In its conception of the relation of religion to life Calvinism was mediaeval, and where Calvinist influence was dominant the development of secularism was long delayed. We see this influence in our own national history in Puritan New England. Even the era of modern science which has so completely changed the mediaeval world outlook, long perpetuated intellectual elements which had a pronounced mediaeval reference. And in political theory the belief in the divine origin of governmental authority seems to have retained a firm grip on the Anglo-Saxon mind through our own Revolutionary era. Little by little, however, the secular drift has engulfed the various phases of modern life and in our time such acknowledgment of spiritual sanctions over temporal affairs as finds expression is vague and unconvincing.

There are those who look upon contemporary secularism and call it emancipation. I am not disposed toward pessimism, nor am I enamored of Puritanism. It may even be admitted that every rigid orthodoxy produces its own antidote and that a stage in cultural development that is characterized by such orthodoxy as persisted through the early years of American history is bound to be followed by what we may call a retreat from belief. Perhaps this is the only way mankind has of correcting its historical excesses. But even if this view be taken the gravity of the situation resulting from such a swing of the pendulum is not minimized thereby. The position here defended is that contemporary secularism marks a deep cleavage in our culture. It has an ill-concealed nostalgic quality. An order of life that restricts the range of those sanctions which have their origin in the spiritual insights of a people and which are expressed in their corporate religious experience could not be free from inner strains and contradictions. Modern society is continually at war with itself. This nation clings to its religious heritage by supporting tremendous religious establishments which it exempts from taxation, by invoking the divine blessing upon its public undertakings, by proclaiming on its coins "In God We Trust," by maintaining the liberty of the most troublesome of its religious sects, by expending huge sums on the maintenance of chaplains in its armed services, and in numerous other ways. Yet in business, industry, politics and education it operates under secular autonomies with a minimum of guidance from the religion to which it claims allegiance.

Nowhere is this inner tension more evident than in the current effort to give power and authority to the democratic ideal. I am less interested than some others in the controversy over the metaphysical basis of democracy. That many persons who manifest a devotion to democracy as a spiritual ideal are wholly unwilling to rest it upon any religious formula is too evident to be disputed. Whether or not the democratic spirit can be permanently maintained by our people as a whole without the conviction of man's spiritual origin which our fathers wrote into the great Declaration cannot be settled by argument. But what matters mightily is that democracy requires for its perfection and preservation a degree of humility and dedication unknown to us which it has always been the function of religion to foster. Again I say, religion is the corporate dedication of life, the heart-searching and penitent reconsecration that comes to fruition when men bow before the Most High. There are those who approach their Holy of Holies with songs and litanies and sacramental symbols and there are those who come into that presence through a sacrament of silence, but man has never learned to discipline his spirit to the extent that sustained moral effort requires without systematic provision for that group experience known as worship. There are, to be sure, many who feel no need to worship, but the combined evidence of experience indicates that they are exceptions. That they may see themselves as prophets of a new "secular" religion, without churches or ceremonial or gods, entitles them to respect for their sincerity but it does not entitle them to credit for having correctly discerned the nature and needs of men. In any case, there is no evidence that they speak for more than a small minority. That the mind of this generation is so largely secularized is not to be taken as evidence that our people have found a new and glorious way into a secular City of Man, any more than the waywardness of the generations with which the prophets of Israel pleaded was evidence that the message of those prophets had become outmoded. Overwhelmingly our secularism is evidence of the lure of the marketplace and the lust of power. Those who claim that the spiritual discipline which the democratic way of life requires can be achieved without the institutions of corporate religion have a grievous burden of proof resting upon them.

This is not to make any bombastic claims for the purity of contemporary religious institutions. As we have already noted, the pressure of a secular environment has in large measure secularized the church itself. Man cannot live permanently in two worlds, one in which he bows humbly and penitently in recognition of his unworthiness and the other in which he lives by the slogan, "Business is business." Until the structure of society is made conducive to a high dedication and a corresponding discipline, religion will be continually degenerating into escape or hypocrisy. If we insist that the remedy for the ills of democracy is more democracy, are we not constrained by the same logic to say that the remedy for the ills of religion is more religion and higher religion? And there is no surer way to render religion ethically and socially inadequate than to build a wall between religion and public education.

This aspect of our subject—the secularization of education—is one that I have elsewhere developed, not without subsequent controversy. In the light of experience I shall attempt to restate what seem to me the essentials of the matter as it confronts American educators.

In the first place, our schools became secularized in response to a critical situation. The common school movement ran counter to the diversification of religion, that is, to sectarianism. The relatively unified public education program which got under way a little over a century ago was totally inconsistent with the teaching of religion in the dogmatic sectarian forms in which it was then taught. Horace Mann had a dream that out of the welter of sectarianism might come a common denominator of religious faith and practice that would vitalize public education. It is a curious fact that this great educator to whose efforts to keep the schools free of religious controversy contemporary defenders of secularization now point, was himself eager that non-sectarian religion find a place in the schools. The divorcement of life from religious sanctions was apparently among the last things he was willing to contemplate. The secularization of public education resulted more directly from the fact of religious sectarianism than from any other cause. How Mann and his contemporaries could have followed any other course under the circumstances in which they found themselves it is difficult now to see. But it is equally difficult to imagine that he would have been content with the situation existing in our time.

It is natural that current concern for a religious orientation in public education should follow Horace Mann's line of thought. Why, it is asked, can we not find a common body of accepted religious truth upon which the various religious bodies will agree and teach that as a foundation for religious faith and life? Many people believe that this is possible and desirable. But such an undertaking, if conceived as offering a minimum of religious beliefs which "all reasonable men" may be expected to accept, is inconsistent, it seems to me, with sound educational theory. How controversial subjects shall be taught in the schools is itself one of the most controversial issues in contemporary education. Take, for instance, the current issue over free enterprise which sharply divides the political mind of the nation. We can state the issue, explain how it arose, set forth pros and cons, but to say "This is the right answer," is beyond the province of public education as most liberal educators would define it. The case is the same with reference to many other questions of public concern.

The fact is that the complexity of modern life and the growing concern for freedom of thought have given rise to a new conception of teaching in matters where "beliefs" are concerned, whether in politics, economics, science, philosophy or religion. There is, of course, a large body of scientific and historical "fact"—that is, a body of conclusions from investigation which is scarcely called in question—concerning which the educator speaks with relative certainty and finality. But in the ever-growing area of hypothesis, of practical judgment and of adventurous faith it is now a mark of maturity to avoid dogmatism as to what other men should believe. It is well, of course, to recognize that education in areas where value judgments are involved inevitably and desirably has an element of persuasion; otherwise purposeful education for living would be a meaningless phrase. But to assume that beliefs about the meaning of life can be fixed by a sort of educational fiat, by submitting propositions to be accepted without question, is to ignore the principle of voluntary, active response which is central in modern educational theory. The mature mind does not take to hand-me-down beliefs. Such beliefs, passively accepted and held, are not the stuff of effective moral conviction.

We seem therefore to be impelled either to continue in our education the dualism of the religious and the "secular," or to incorporate the study of religion as we do other phases of the culture in which conflicts in belief and moral judgment are encountered. If education is induction into life within a given culture, the school program should aim to produce intelligent sensitivity to all the major interests and activities of the community. The social studies program exists for just this purpose. It is, I believe, preeminently the place to bring religion into the purview of education. I say this not only because the aim of the social studies is to enable the student to understand contemporary life in its entirety but because, as I have already pointed out, religion is primarily a form of corporate behavior which can no more be studied adequately out of books than art or politics. The major fault of the public schools in respect to religion is not that they eschew dogma but that they prevent the growing child from acquiring a working knowledge of a major aspect of contemporary institutional life and from doing this as a part of his general education. To object that this will expose young minds to controversy, is to offer the same objection that has impeded the progress of the social studies in the political and economic spheres. However, I think it very doubtful that a wise and sincere effort to promote the study of contemporary religion as a part of the social studies program will, save in exceptional instances, precipitate anything like as much controversy as has been engendered recently by the study of economic and political problems.

Along with the study of religion on this empirical basis should go the study of the major religious classics as part of the literary treasures of our culture. To assume that religious literature cannot be taught without turning it into dogma is to impugn the entire humanities program in public education. The religious classics make the same claim for selective educational use that is made by the "secular" classics. The same criteria apply: do they aid in an understanding of man's life, and do they enrich the experience of a growing person?

At one point—and it is one of major importance—the opponents of including religion in the study program of tax-supported schools seem to be peculiarly inconsistent. They see no impropriety in setting the educational stage for propagating doctrines that are bitterly resented by religious groups because they deny essential tenets of their faith. I have seen more trouble grow out of indoctrination from the instructor's desk aimed *against* traditional religious assumptions, in the name of philosophy, than I have seen growing out of the *affirmation* of religious dogmas. Now I am personally willing that academic freedom be construed as covering attacks upon even the most cherished religious beliefs. I feel better to have teachers free to make extreme statements—perhaps wild statements—if they are sincere. But by what possible logic does the convinced naturalist or experimentalist claim the right to denounce supernaturalism and then insist that religious subject matter has no place in public education? At one jump he has landed in the midst of religious controversy. If some very crude form of religious teaching appears widely in the schools, will not the ardent critics of religious traditions, who claim special educational privileges, be in large part responsible?

On the other hand exponents of religion will not improve its status in the thinking of educators or hasten its recognition in the school program if they insist that religious insight is a substitute for scientific inquiry or that factual statements put forward in the name of religion are exempt from scientific scrutiny. Religion as well as education will profit by the abandonment of the modern dualism that has thrust them apart.

TRENDS IN RELIGIOUS THOUGHT THAT AFFECT SOCIAL OUTLOOK

By

PAUL J. TILLICH, Ph.D.

Professor of Philosophical Theology, Union Theological Seminary

Religious thought is able to affect social outlook, because religion is our relation to what concerns us ultimately. Religion at its center is ultimate, unconditional, inescapable concern. Therefore, religion is the expression of the meaning of our life as a whole. It is related to every realm of human existence. Religion is not a province beside other provinces of the human mind. It is never "beside" not even in the sense of "above." It is the ultimate concern in all preliminary concerns, the center of all theoretical and practical activities, the inexhaustible meaning in everything that has meaning. Religious thought can influence social outlook, because religious thought deals with the ultimate meaning of man's social existence as much as it deals with the ultimate meaning of man's scientific, moral, political, aesthetic existence. It cannot be separated from any of them, because religious thought deals with existence as such. Only as this basic and inclusive concept of religion is recognized, can the relation of religion to the social realm be described adequately.

But after the first and affirmative answer to the question has been stated, a second and restrictive answer must follow. Religion has not only the fundamental and universal meaning just mentioned, but it also has a derived and particular meaning, namely, a system of symbols, actions and emotions in which the meaning of our existence is expressed. Religion in this secondary sense, for instance, an organized church, is a separate realm and cannot claim authority over the special structures of the other realms. Therefore religion as a special sphere of human existence—although based on the ultimate meaning of all human existence—should not try to interfere with the other spheres. It should not try to exercise scientific or artistic or economic or political authority. If it does so the other spheres revolt against it, as they did at the end of the Middle Ages, and thus religion is deprived of its central and all embracing significance. Church interference is not the answer to the question of the relation between religion and the social order.

A third answer must be found, uniting the universal affirmative character of the first one with the restrictive character of the second one. Religious thought can influence social outlook by showing the ultimate meaning of human existence and the presupposition of its realization in human nature and destiny. It is much too narrow to restrict the import of religion to the ethical implications of social life. They themselves are based on an interpretation of man and his world. Without such an interpretation social as well as ethical demands and purposes are without a ground and norm. Without a basic understanding of human finiteness and tragedy, of historical time and the nature of the historical process, of the interdependence of personality and community, of the relation between nature and history, between body and mind, between reason and the irrational—without these no social program has a lasting significance.

The basic definition of religion as ultimate concern implies that religious thought cannot be separated from philosophy. All methodical thought has philosophical presuppositions and philosophy, if it is more than an academic matter, must ask for the meaning of being in general and of human existence in particular. It does so upon assumptions and by means which differ from the ways of religious thought. But it cannot avoid the question of the ultimate. In this sense genuine philosophy has a religious character, not by intention but by implication, and cannot be separated from other forms of religious thought.

It seems to me most adequate to distinguish the different types of religious thought which affect social outlook by their different interpretations of the nature of man. The nature of man can be understood first in terms of his essential, created character—

mythologically speaking, of his original goodness. The nature of man can be understood secondly in terms of his existential, self-determined character—mythologically speaking, of his distortion by the fall. Only in man is this dual consideration possible, because only man has the freedom which enables him to contradict his own essential goodness. Human freedom necessitates the distinction between man's essential and existential nature. The nature of man can be understood, thirdly, in terms of a permanent conflict between his essential and his existential nature—mythologically speaking, of the process of his salvation. From this threefold interpretation of human nature follow three possibilities of religious thought affecting the social outlook:

1) A type of religious thought which emphasizes man's essential nature and neglects the existential distortion of it

2) A type of religious thought which emphasizes man's existential situation and neglects his essential goodness

3) A type of religious thought which emphasizes the tension between man's essential goodness and his existential distortion.

Each of these types of religious thought has special consequences for the social outlook.

I

If man's essential nature is emphasized over against man's existential distortion, mankind is considered to be a part of nature, developing like nature from potentiality to actuality. On this view history is the actualization of human potentialities. Many things are not yet actualized but they will be in the progress of history. The "not yet," the shortcomings in the historical self-realization of human nature, are natural and will be progressively eliminated. In a process of emergent evolution man will reach the stage in which his essential possibilities are realized. There is a providential harmony between the free will of man (which could disturb the course of natural evolution) and the development of the whole. In the long run man will actualize all his potentialities under the guidance of God Who is interpreted as the moral world order, or the progressive synthesis of the elements of being and value, or the creative ideal of goodness. Although the individual man is free to oppose the general progress and to frustrate possibilities of a creative synthesis in himself and in others, the progressive development as a whole is guaranteed. All human potentialities will be actualized in the process of history. Divine Providence—philosophically speaking, the preestablished harmony between the individual and the whole—is the guarantee of the progressive synthesis.

Man, for this type of theological thought, is essentially intact. Reason, his determining and distinguishing quality, is not distorted, at least not in principle. There is, of course, a gap between man's high bodily and low spiritual perfection; there were and there still are infantile stages in man's development; persistent difficulties attend man's effort to adapt himself mentally and socially to the structure of our world. But this handicap is not insurmountable. In many respects it already has been overcome and it certainly will be entirely overcome in a not indefinitely remote future. The history of mankind is a long educational process in which man's rational possibilities will become increasingly realized. The history of religion is a process of cumulative experience in which ever higher truths and values are realized. God is the driving power toward the victory of reason over pure nature within man and outside of him. Christ is an outstanding, perhaps the outstanding agency of Divine Providence.

This is the theological attitude of bourgeois humanism, since the Renaissance discovered the greatness of man's essential nature and Erasmus defended human freedom against Luther's doctrine of human bondage. This is the theology of the leaders of Deism and Enlightenment, of the German classical philosophers and poets, including Schleiermacher and Hegel. This is the doctrine of Ritschl, of the theology of the Social Gospel, of moralistic theism and so-called theological humanism. In spite of the differences between these theologians and philosophers of religion, they all represent an interpretation of essential life which is based on the belief in the integrity of man's rational nature.

The social outlook which follows from this type of theology is strongly interrelated with the development of modern bourgeois society, of which it is the ideological self-interpretation. Bourgeois society has developed in three main stages in which the bourgeoisie is seen as successfully attacking, controlling and defending. The social outlook was different in each of these stages and so was the attitude toward religion and Christianity. The fighting bourgeoisie had a strong feeling for its historical vocation. The period of reason, the final aim of history has begun. Man has become in principle what he essentially is—mature in his reason. The infantile and adolescent stages of the long "prehistory" of mankind are past. Real history, namely the development of man on the basis of mature rationality has begun with the rise of an enlightened bourgeoisie. Religious symbols which do not fit into this new self-interpretation of man are superstitious remnants of the youth of mankind. They must be dismissed or transformed. The age of autonomy and rational self-determination is at hand. Liberal politics, democratic procedures and progressive education have become possible. Their application will bring to perfection what in principle is given: Man's rational maturity.

In the period of the victorious bourgeoisie the social outlook became less revolutionary and more evolutionary. The belief in reason became less enthusiastic and more sober, more scientific and finally more technical. The fighting reason was replaced by the calculating reason. Progress was slowed down by a large amount of political and social conservatism. The ruling bourgeoisie is afraid of the revolutionary impetus of its fighting period. It can accept more of the traditional religious symbols, using them as a helpful ideology for the masses which are not supposed to know that the enlightened leaders themselves do not believe any more in traditional religion. But this does not prevent the theologians of this period from demanding and hoping for an increase in enlightenment, liberalism, democracy, peace and universal justice. The pursuit of individual interest will not seriously hamper the growing world community; on the contrary, it will be the way to foster it. Pacifism and the Social Gospel are the most important movements representing the social outlook of this period.

When it became apparent that the contradictions within the assumed system of harmonic development were so profound that they practically disrupted the harmony, the third stage of bourgeois society started, the stage of defense and decay. The basic presupposition, man's essential integrity, was still maintained. But the belief that the period of rational maturity already has been reached was given up. A new start, after a revolutionary transformation, is held to be necessary. The substantial advance in theory is frustrated by the slight advance in practice—in social practice, as Marxism emphasized; in personal practice, as the doctrine of man since Nietzsche and Freud has shown. The utopian forms of early Religious Socialism made the same point, identifying the proletarian revolution with the coming of the Kingdom of God. Although these ideas did not transcend the bourgeois frame of thought, especially the interpretation of man's nature by Renaissance and Enlightenment, they prepared the breaking of that frame by making manifest the contradictions within it.

II

The second type of theology, opposing the first, denies that there is any approach to man's essential nature, either because it does not exist or because it has been lost completely. The former possibility is represented by pessimistic naturalism, the latter by pessimistic supranaturalism. Both forms of this theology have made their appearance in great strength in connection with the disintegration of bourgeois society in its third stage. And both forms had a tremendous influence on social outlook.

Naturalistic pessimism developed very early as the inescapable shadow of rationalism. Again and again the leaders of Enlightenment and the profounder spirits of the nineteenth century questioned the optimistic presupposition that there is a harmony between nature and reason, that rational progress is rooted in the nature of things, be it called Divine Providence or pre-established harmony. If we look into the depths of human nature we discover irrational and even antirational forces such as will to power, cupidity, will to death, destructiveness, anxiety and despair. If we look into the depths of man's social existence we discover a cruel fight for survival in the masses and a brutal conquest and maintenance of power in the ruling classes. We discover an unimaginable amount of individual and social suffering and we are inclined to replace the progressivist by a tragic interpretation of human life. This naturalistic pessimism expresses itself in half-theological philosophies or a purely individualistic, will-to-power philosophy. It is the attitude which supports the present attack on the traditional religions and their systems of value. For the quasi-theology of naturalistic pessimism man is neither intact nor distorted. He is as he is, no essential perfection can be posited over against his real existence.

The social outlook following from this type of naturalistic theology is determined by the unrestricted acceptance of the power principle. Instead of Divine Providence which guarantees social progress, different and changing powers, aristocracies, nations, races, cultures, classes, control the incalculable course of history. Liberal and democratic ideas are weapons in the hands of the rulers as long as they can use them and will be discarded in favor of authoritarian systems as soon as they become weapons in the hands of the ruled masses. No rational structure of society is possible, reason can only be used as technical reason in the hands of the powerful groups in order to subject nature and society to their purposes. These are the social consequences of a doctrine of man which denies man's essential goodness.

They are very similar to the social outlook of the supranaturalistic form of theological pessimism which largely agrees with the naturalistic form with respect to man's actual situation, i. e., his existential nature. The same tragic contradictions in human existence to which pessimistic naturalism refers are emphasized in this type of theological thinking. Such concepts as anxiety, despair and melancholy are emphasized most forcefully by people like Kierkegaard and his contemporary followers. They all agree in a tragic, non-progressivist interpretation of history. The story of the "Tower of Babel" is used as the symbol of the tragic impossibility that mankind ever will reach political and cultural unity. On all these points both forms of pessimism agree. The main difference is that the supranaturalistic form affirms the loss of man's essential nature, its paradoxical restitution in the Christian event and its fragmentary visibility in the message of the Christian Church. But this does not refer to the social and cultural life outside the Church. No approach to essential manhood is possible through reason. Therefore no rational system of life can be expected. In spite of the revealed integrity of man's nature in Jesus as the Christ, no historical integrity or progress toward integrity can be imagined. The fulfilment is transcendent only. The Kingdom of God has nothing to do with history. History is left to man in his existential distortion and to the demonic powers controlling him.

The social outlook of this theology is not very different from that of pessimistic naturalism. The principle of power is interpreted as a consequence of human sin and is justified as a means of suppressing sin. Rational criteria to be applied against an existing state do not exist. The irrational power of the government must be acknowledged, even if it is destructive. Revolution is prohibited and in vain, because man's existential nature cannot be changed. So pessimistic supranaturalism betrays a very conservative character; it has no belief in social progress at all. It is interesting to note that Luther's pessimistic supranaturalism very early was compared to Machiavelli's pessimistic naturalism. Political absolutism could use the one as well as the other. Today Karl Barth's pessimistic supranaturalism has helped to destroy the Religious-Socialist attempts in pre-Hitler Germany to stop Nazism by creating a better social order on the basis of Christian principles. And even when Barth became a fanatical anti-Nazi he showed in his letter to the British Christians that it was not the common fight of people of all religions and creeds against the National-Socialist distortion of humanity that interested him, but the defense of the Church as the finger pointing only to heaven and not to earth. He challenges the British Christians to interpret the war in terms of secular humanism and not of religious transcendence. He, like all pessimistic supranaturalists, is not interested in history as such nor in a social transformation for the sake of humanity.

III

The third type of theology attempts a dialectical union of the first and the second type. It presupposes, on the one hand, the essential goodness of human nature; but it denies that human existence is a natural process in which his essential nature is gradually actualized. It presupposes, on the other hand, the existential distortion of human nature; but it denies that human existence is a natural process without the critical and promising presence of essential goodness. Man's essential nature is neither a mere ideology nor a merely transcendent possibility, but it is actual in history. It is not lacking or completely destroyed, but it is fragmentarily and ambiguously visible. Human history is neither a mere progress nor a mere tragedy, but it is a fight between the forces of perfection and those of distortion. The belief in Providence means that in this struggle the negative forces cannot ultimately prevail; but it does not guarantee any kind of harmonious progress. It gives the certainty that the victory over man's existential distortion is won from the point of view of eternity; but it does not give the certainty that there is or will be a victory at any point of history.

There are three main forms of this type, the social outlook of which is important for our present situation—Catholicism, Ecumenical Protestantism, and Dialectical Religious Socialism.

Roman Catholic theology emphasizes the large amount of essential goodness and rationality remaining in mankind after the fall of the first man. Although man's freedom and natural perfection are corrupted, they are not thoroughly distorted. Only the original supranatural gift of community with God is lost. But this was an addition to his essential goodness. Its loss means a weakening, but not an extinction of the divine image in man. Consequently man is able to prepare himself for the reception of grace. And grace, when received, is able to restore the integrity of human nature and reason in a process of progressive sanctification.

The social consequences of the Catholic doctrine of man are as dialectical as the picture of man itself is. On the basis of man's corrupted nature Catholicism acknowledges the principle of power and supports the earthly authorities. In this respect it often approximates the attitude of pessimistic supranaturalism. On the basis of man's preserved rationality Catholicism can accept liberal and democratic forms of life. In this respect it often approximates the theology of optimistic rationality. A balance between the two trends is permanently achieved by the Church and its authoritarian hierarchy on the basis of the restitution of the divine grace which was lost in the fall. Therefore the Church is the central factor in every social outlook of Roman Catholicism. The Church can favor power politics in a special situation and it can favor liberal politics in another situation. The criterion is always the ethical doctrines and political influence of the Church. This excludes Fascist totalitarianism as well as humanistic liberalism. A system in which the Church is not the central factor can be tolerated in terms of compromise but it cannot be accepted as true. There can be no doubt that the present world situation and the breakdown of autonomous Liberalism as well as of totalitarian Fascism offers an unexpected opportunity to the social outlook of Catholic theology.

The second form in which a dialectical union of the first and the second type of present theology is achieved is the theology of Ecumenical Protestantism. An ecumenical theology as a special theological method does not exist; but there are trends visible in all ecumenical thinking that justify the conception of an ecumenical theology. The ecumenical movement is a result of the fact that since the beginning of our century "world" in the historical sense has been established. World traffic and world economy were its presuppositions. World wars are its first actualization. A world union of the churches is its ideal projection. The unity of the Church as the "Assembly of God" or as the "Body of Christ" has always been emphasized—as much as the essential unity of mankind. But today "world" also means the historical-empirical unity of all nations in their interdependence. And "Church" should also mean the historical-empirical unity of all churches in their collaboration.

The ecumenical movement was started in the Anglo-Saxon countries under the strong influence of their missionary activities. It has slowly grasped the Continental churches, where the Continental Lutherans were most reluctant. The collaboration of the Greek Orthodox churches has slightly balanced American denominationalism, but the theological trends which have appeared up to now are essentially Protestant in origin and nature. They show two poles corresponding to the two main theological types we have distinguished. The one pole is represented by American progressivist optimism, the other by Continental tragic pessimism. The Anglican church mediates somewhat between the two poles, providing leadership which appreciates the dynamic impulses coming from the progressivist mood of America as much as the restraining reflections coming from the tragic mood of Europe.

The social outlook of Ecumenical Protestantism has found a very profound, radical and inclusive expression in the statements of the Oxford Conference, some of which show the spirit of a theological vanguard. But on the whole the social outlook of the ecumenical movement does not transcend very far the ideals of Anglo-Saxon democracy in the direction of a strongly social interpretation. The function of the churches according to these programs is not that of the Catholic Church, to balance authoritatively the different social forces. The ecumenical churches are supposed to influence indirectly, by teaching, example, spiritual power, temporal movements and authorities. They expect that the present world situation, especially the reaction against Fascist authoritarianism, will favor the non-Catholic churches at least as much as Roman Catholicism—if they are able to understand the general trend toward a new collectivism.

This condition of the effectiveness of the social outlook of ecumenical theology points to the remaining form of our third type of theology: Dialectical Religious Socialism. It is distinguished from the different utopian forms of Socialism generally and non-dialectical

Religious Socialism in particular by accepting the pessimistic view of human existence emphasized by the second type of theology. But it is distinguished from the tragic interpretation of history by its revolutionary activism, and the element of progressivist feeling implied in every revolutionary action.

Religious Socialism in its dialectical form has largely accepted the Marxian analysis of bourgeois capitalism, while rejecting many philosophical doctrines of Marx and his followers. Main emphasis is laid on Marx's description of the dehumanization and alienation of man in the later stages of bourgeois society. This description is confirmed by an analysis of the present situation in all realms of human existence. Dialectical Religious Socialism has developed a theology the social outlook of which is not an accidental consequence but an essential element. Human existence is interpreted with reference to the concrete social existence of our period. Historical concreteness and universal validity are united. On this basis a religious interpretation of history is given, which tries to avoid utopianism as well as historical indifference. It believes in the *Kairos,* the right moment of time, in which eternity breaks into history and demands a decisive step, without assuming that this step will lead into an immanent or transcendent stage of perfection. The doctrine of the *Kairos* unites in a special way theological optimism and pessimism and overcomes the alternative.

Dialectical Religious Socialism is not represented by a powerful group or a mass movement. It is the attitude of small groups all over the world. Neither the churches nor labor movements nor political parties are the representatives of Religious Socialism. But there are individuals everywhere who understand the signs of our time and who have a social outlook on the basis of a more developed theology. It is my conviction, that neither the Catholic Church nor Ecumenical Protestantism but the spirit of these small groups will determine the future of mankind.

RELIGIOUS LIBERTY IN THE POSTWAR WORLD

By

LUTHER A. WEIGLE, Ph.D.

Dean of the Divinity School, Yale University

In his *History of Freedom of Thought,* published in 1913, Professor J. B. Bury said: "The struggle of reason against authority has ended in what now appears to be a decisive and permanent victory for liberty." But within a few months the First World War began. In view of what has happened since, Bury's statement merely reveals the fallibility of academic thinking. He was so obsessed by the idea that the church has been the enemy of freedom of thought and speech that it occurred to him only as a remote and improbable possibility that the state might again deny freedom of conscience and undertake the coercion of the human mind. It did not occur to him at all, so far as we may infer from the pages of the book, that the church and the forces of religious faith might stand on the side of freedom.

Yet both of these possibilities have come to pass. The tyranny of the totalitarian state threatens to put an end to human freedom; and in many countries moral conscience and faith in God have inspired resistance to the forces that would enslave the human spirit.

If the totalitarian powers win the present war, there will be no religious liberty. This is not only because of the general control of the whole of life which totalitarianism enforces, but because there are especial points of conflict between it and free religion. Totalitarianism exalts the state itself to the position of deity, repudiates the relevance to the state of the moral law, viciously persecutes the Jewish people, and denounces Christianity as a religion fit only for the soft and weak.

Our discussion of religious liberty in the postwar world, therefore, must be based upon the assumption that the United Nations will win. It is possible, of course, that there may be victory for neither side, with the war leading to a negotiated peace. So far as we can see, however, which is admittedly not very far, the principles of liberty for which the United Nations stand will be the same in either case. The difference would lie in their power and responsibility to make full provision for liberty in accordance with these principles.

It should be said at once that victory for the United Nations will not of itself assure religious freedom, any more than it will assure economic justice. These need to be achieved. Victory for the United Nations will keep open the possibility of achieving a more free and more just civilization, under the new conditions of technology, communication and transport; whereas a victory for the totalitarian powers would close this possibility until their tragic experiment shall have burned itself out.

It should be said, too, that it is possible that the problem of religious liberty may not take a large place in the discussions of those who draw up the conditions of peace. This may be because there is so much agreement as to the broad general principle; or it may be because there is so much disagreement as to the specific meanings and applications of that principle.

In the discussions incident to the drafting of the Covenant of the League of Nations, President Wilson twice and Lord Robert Cecil once presented written clauses against the inequitable treatment of minorities and interference with religion or discrimination against the adherents of any particular creed, religion, or belief. But neither of Wilson's proposed articles was included in the agreed draft brought forward by the British and American delegations, which is the basis of the Covenant. Cecil's clause, proposed at a later stage, was eventually rejected by a very large majority, neither the British nor the American delegation finally voting for its inclusion.

It is probable that more attention than this will be given to the problem of religious liberty by the future Peace Conference. Among the reasons for this are: (1) the fact that the fate of minorities has been so poignant an issue in recent years, and these minorities have in most cases been marked by some religious distinction; (2) the fact that the anti-Jewish, anti-Christian, pagan ideology and propaganda of the totalitarian powers have spawned a generation that must be reeducated; (3) the general recognition of the need for deepening the bonds of mutual understanding and respect that are drawing the United Nations together, in order that the foundations of world order may be well and truly laid. It is not without practical significance that President Roosevelt included freedom of religion as one of the four freedoms for which we fight: freedom of speech and of religion, freedom from want and from fear.

The United Nations agree in professing adherence to the general principle of religious freedom, but they differ in various matters of policy with respect to religion. Great Britain, Norway, the Netherlands, and other European governments have each an established state church; the United States of America has no such established church. In most of the Latin-American countries Roman Catholicism is the established religion of the state. Russia has made atheism the official position; has a constitution which permits freedom of religious worship and of anti-religious propaganda; has pushed this propaganda hard, and has not refrained from religious persecution, but has had to compromise with the seemingly ineradicable religious disposition of the Russian people. The people of China profess the practical faith that has been theirs through the centuries; but the Christian movement in China is growing steadily in strength and has contributed far beyond its proportionate numbers to the determination of public policy.

In the Constitution of the United States, the principle of religious freedom is embodied in two clauses. Article 6, Section III, contains as its last clause the provision that "no religious test shall ever be required as a qualification to any office of public trust under the United States." The first amendment reads "Congress shall make no law respecting the establishment of religion or prohibiting the free exercise thereof." The constitutions of all the states contain similar statements guaranteeing the general rights of conscience in phrases such as: "every man may worship God according to his own conscience." "The free enjoyment of all religious sentiments and the different modes of worship shall ever be held sacred." "It is the duty of the Legislature to pass suitable laws to protect every religious community in the peaceable enjoyment of its own mode of worship." "No human authority or law ought in any case whatever, to control or interfere with the rights of conscience in matters of religion." "No person ought to be molested in person or estate on account of his religious persuasion."

Justice Cooley's exposition of the principle of religious freedom, in his authoritative work on *Constitutional Limitations,* states the following to be things which are not lawful under any of the American constitutions:

1. Any law respecting an establishment of religion. The legislatures have not been left at liberty to effect a union of church and state, or to establish preferences by law in favor of any one religious persuasion or mode of worship.

2. Compulsory support, by taxation or otherwise, of religious instruction.

3. Compulsory attendance upon religious worship.

4. Restraints upon the free exercise of religion according to the dictates of the conscience.

5. Restraints upon the expression of religious belief.

Three recent pronouncements of Christian bodies may be quoted as representative of public opinion in Great Britain and America. The first is a resolution of the Conference of Presbyterian Churches of Great Britain and Ireland held in Edinburgh, January 28, 1942: "Recognizing that liberty of conscience is an essential part of civil liberty and that the free exchange of religious convictions is a necessary condition of all understanding between races and nations, the Conference urges on all governments the recognition of the unfettered right of every individual to a free choice in religious faith and to the public profession and preaching of it, so long as these faiths do not run counter to law and order."

The Study Conference on the Bases of a Just and Durable Peace held at Delaware, Ohio, March 3–5, 1942, stated as the ninth of its

Guiding Principles: "We believe that the right of all men to pursue work of their own choosing and to enjoy security from want and oppression is not limited by race, color or creed. The rights and liberties of racial and religious minorities in all lands should be recognized and safeguarded. Freedom of religious worship, of speech and assembly, of the press, and of scientific inquiry and teaching are fundamental to human development and in keeping with the moral order."

In *The Christian Church and World Order,* a statement issued on May 7, 1942, by the (British) Commission of the Churches for International Friendship and Social Responsibility, under the chairmanship of the Archbishop of Canterbury, appears the following: "Religious freedom must include, both for individuals and for organized bodies, liberty to worship, preach and teach according to conviction, the right of public witness, and freedom to bring up children in the faith of their parents; and it should definitely include the right of individuals to enter or leave a religious community or to transfer from one to another, for a man has no true religious freedom if he is free only to remain in the religious community in which he was born. In order that such freedom should not impinge upon the rights and liberties of others, it should be subject to a reasonable interpretation of public order and to generally accepted moral standards; and no legal penalty or disability should be attached to membership or non-membership of any religious community."

Among secular groups, I may quote from a Statement of American Proposals for a New World Order, issued June 6, 1941, for the consideration of the American people by the Commission to Study the Organization of Peace, headed by Professor James T. Shotwell: "Democracy, by its very principles, must concede to each nation the form of government which its people desire subject to the assurance by law of standards of individual liberty within each nation, and subject to an international guarantee against aggression by any nation. We hold that an international Bill of Rights, with such guarantees, is an indispensable basis of our own peace and security." The document goes on to advocate guarantees for social, religious, and political minorities, for the sake of peace.

The Federal Council of the Churches of Christ in America, together with the International Missionary Council, has organized a committee which is at work, studying the problem of the specific application of the principle of religious freedom, in the light of recent experience in the various countries of the world. Its aim is "(1) to formulate for presentation to the British, American, and possibly other sympathetic governments, a memorandum of *desiderata* in religious and missionary liberties, which should be duly considered in the reorganization of international agreements and of national systems that is expected at the close of the war; (2) to provide a framework in which particular and national problems of religious liberty may be seen in world perspective by those who must cope with them in limited settings."

Without knowing what *desiderata* are emerging in the course of the committee's inquiry, I shall list some of the more important rights that may be claimed in the name of religious freedom. This list is tentative only. But it may serve as a basis for discussion; it will certainly serve to show how complex the problem is. The rights may be grouped in three classes: (1) the religious freedom of the individual; (2) the religious freedom of the church or congregation; (3) the religious freedom of citizens.

I. The religious freedom of the individual includes the following rights:

1. To believe as reason and conscience dictate. The terms "reason" and "conscience" are used, here and throughout this list, not as opposed to "revelation," but as denoting the human response to divine revelation.

2. To worship God in the ways which reason and conscience deem appropriate.

3. To live and to act in accordance with such belief and worship.

4. To express religious belief in speech. This includes all forms of expression—art, journalism, books, the radio, etc., as well as oral speech.

5. To express religious belief for the purpose of persuasion, to

convince and convert others. This includes all forms of religious propaganda. It is the human side of Christian evangelism.

6. To educate his children in his religious faith (including both belief and action).

7. To join with others in the organized life and work of a church, congregation, or other religious fellowship.

8. To withdraw from such affiliation with a religious organization or community; and, at the constraint of reason and conscience, to change belief, with corresponding changes in worship, action, speech, education, and affiliation.

9. To disbelieve in God, to deny religion, and to act, speak, persuade, educate, and affiliate with others in ways appropriate to this disbelief or atheism.

II. By the term "church" we designate not only a local congregation, but also national, supranational, and ecumenical bodies. With this understanding,

The religious freedom of the church or congregation includes the following rights:

1. To assemble for unhindered public worship.

2. To organize for the more effective conduct and perpetuation of religious belief, worship and action.

3. To determine its own constitution, polity, and conditions of membership.

4. To determine its own faith and creed—free from imposition by the state or any other group.

5. To determine its own forms of worship—free from imposition by the state or any other group.

6. To encourage and facilitate action by its members in accordance with its belief and worship.

7. To bear witness, preach, teach, persuade, and seek commitment or conversion.

8. To determine the qualifications of its ministers, and to educate, ordain, and maintain an adequate ministry.

9. To educate both children and adults. This affirmation of the right of the church or congregation to educate does not deny or exclude the right of the state to educate.

10. To hold property and secure support for its work.

11. To cooperate or to unite with other churches or congregations.

12. Finally, the principle of religious freedom requires that these rights of the church or congregation be similarly the rights of organized groups of unbelievers or atheists.

III. The religious freedom of citizens includes:

1. The right of the citizen to hold the state itself responsible to the moral law and to God; and the right to labor to this end through appropriate judgments, witness, and constructive participation in the activities of citizenship.

2. The right of the citizen to dissent in the name of religious belief (reason and conscience) from an act or requirement of the state, and to express this dissent in action or in refusal to act as well as in speech. This is the right of so-called conscientious objection. It is recognized that the state may rightfully require a penalty for such dissent, but the penalty for such behavior on grounds of conscience should take these grounds into account.

These freedoms are the right, not only of individual citizens, but also of churches and congregations, so far as these are made up of citizens. They are the right, not only of believers, but also of nonbelievers and atheists.

There are limitations, of course, upon what may be done in the name of religion. The principle of religious freedom does not excuse acts of licentiousness or acts contrary to public order or to generally accepted moral standards, or justify practices inconsistent with the rights of others or with the peace and safety of the state.

The truth is that religious freedom is not a special privilege which the state accords to folk of peculiar temper. It is a right which has entered into the very making of the state. It is one of the basic freedoms in any sound Bill of Rights. Historically, logically, and in practice, it undergirds and sustains human democracy. Without it, all other freedoms are in danger.

The separation of church and state is a sound principle, but one that is much misunderstood. It means that church and state are mutually free, and that neither may rightfully control the other. It does not mean that the state acknowledges no God, or that the state is exempt from the moral law wherewith God sets the bounds of justice for nations as well as for individuals.

It is a commonplace of history that every religious group stands for freedom when it finds its own liberty impaired. The question today is whether all who believe in God will stand together for the freedom of all mankind.

To that question a mighty, worldwide affirmative answer is in the making. The sufferings of the Jews have awakened new sympathy among Christians. Catholics and Protestants have come closer in many parts of the world, as they face together the peril of pagan totalitarianism; and there is ground for hope that the Roman Church may no longer claim religious freedom when it is in the minority but deny religious freedom when it exerts control. The deepseated religious faith of the Russian people has not perished, and their indomitable courage has begun to dispel misgivings about them. China acknowledges with gratitude the contributions of Christian missions to her emancipation.

In the list of rights claimed in the name of religious freedom, I have not made a separate classification of rights involved in the conduct of missions. That is not for lack of belief in missions; it is rather because the right to conduct missions is implied in all of the basic rights which we have named. It is not the special privilege of a favored group or race. It is involved in that free exchange of ideas and personalities which is essential to the progress of the world in freedom, in understanding, and in friendship.

RELIGION AND DEMOCRACY

By

FRANCIS J. McCONNELL, D.D.

Bishop of the Methodist Church

The theme is religion and democracy. I am not going to undertake a definition of democracy. There may be certain things which I will say that will be a kind of description of certain phases of it, but suppose we take our start from the expression, "Democracy is a way of life." That is very general, I know, but that is just by way of introduction.

Any way of life for an individual or a group is necessarily influenced by the conceptions which the person, or persons, have toward the powers which they think of as essentially divine powers. The farther down we go in the scale of civilization, the more directly we see the action of these supposed powers. If you go into Africa today, for example, you will find, if you get outside the circle of foreign influence, the most effective controlling agency in the life of the community is the witch doctor, and the witch doctor, as you know, when he is out of reach of European authorities, has the power of life and death. His power is supposed to be a magic kind of power that gives him control over, influence upon, or intimacy with the forces that we think of as divine. All along the line, from that kind of life on up to the highest type of civilization, we find this dependence on what are thought of at least as higher powers. It may be regretted, it is regretted, that the higher up we get, the weaker this dependence appears in particular circumstances, but nevertheless the dependence is there.

We think of various definitions of democracy, and these forms of definition have different shades of emphasis. I think of the definition given by Abraham Lincoln. I do not know that he meant it to be a definition, but he used the phrase that we all use, government of the people, for the people, and by the people. His emphasis is on the idea of humanity, the people. He got that definition in part from Theodore Parker. It has sometimes been stated that the definition is not original with Lincoln, because he took it from Theodore Parker, but he took it from Theodore Parker with a change.

Theodore Parker's definition was, government of or over all the people for all the people and by all the people. The idea that Lincoln had was that of dealing with essential humanity, with people, and the idea that Parker had was that democracy was something into which he wanted to get *all* the people—an inclusive idea. There is some change in the emphasis. Lincoln dropped out the word "all" in the three phrases with a purpose in mind. He was thinking not of extent merely, but of essential humanity which does include, of course, all men.

Then we have to remember to be on our guard against identifying democracy with any kind of democratic procedure and technique—any one particular kind, I mean. For example, I do not know that you could say that either England or America is at the very top in democratic form of government. There are differences. Probably the two are about equally democratic, but one feature of our system is the election of our highest official for a period of four years. The Prime Minister corresponds to the American President. He is not limited to a term. It depends on the will of the people how long he can go without getting a vote of lack of confidence.

These are mere details. If we look at the things that we think of as essential in our way of life, we say, first of all, as far as the individual is concerned, democracy means, or at least implies, that the individual is an end in himself. That conception of the worth of the individual has not come wholly out of religion. It has been reinterpreted by religion time and time again, and there is, of course, a religious element in it. The conception has been helped on by changes in political economy, and by actual processes in society.

One increase of liberty, one freeing of the individual, has come through the change from the old feudal system to a system of money economy, making money the instrument of larger freedom rather than tying a person down to a particular kind of service. Then, as far as America is concerned, her greatness has not been just that our Constitution was, as Gladstone said, a great work struck off at once by the hand of man, but it has been due to new territory, the opening up of frontiers, which continued until comparatively recent times. However, fundamentally, down under it all is this idea of the worth of a man on the man's own account, and I shall try, in a moment, to show that that is essential to democracy.

Kant said in his great philosophical statement, as you know, that man is not to be considered as a mere tool in any other man's hands, that he is an end in himself, and without his own consent he cannot be used by another man as an instrument. That runs clear back, of course, to the meaning and implication of the teaching of the prophets. If any of the Mosaic laws preceded the teaching of the prophets, with their emphasis on human rights and on human welfare, those emphases, back in those early days even before the prophets, were contributing elements in bringing into the consciousness of the race the sense of the worth of a man on his own account.

That is one side of it. It has been taken very often just in a negative way, that liberty means freedom from external constraint, that no man has a right in any way to restrain the liberty of any other man; but that is purely negative. At the present time, the emphasis that we hear is that if we are going to take an individual as an end in himself and admit him into our social system on that basis, we have to keep in mind that the aim of society, the aim of individual effort, is positive. It is the development of human possibilities at their largest and best. We have to think of the aim of democracy as being not merely keeping our hands off another man, but making it possible, so far as we can, for men to attain to the largest and best possibilities.

Abraham Lincoln once said—I am quoting him again simply because he is looked on as a prophet of democracy—that no man who ever lived is good enough to own another man. Of course, we came long since to that idea as far as outright slavery is concerned, but there is also an obligation on society to see that individuals get their chance at the largest and best development. While a man is to be taken as an end in himself by other men, no man has a right to take himself as an end; that is to say, to live a selfish life for his own development. He has to keep in mind other people, and that brings us to the social side, the relation of the individual to his fellows round about. One danger has been, as we have thought of the progress of democracy in the world, just this: that men have thought it a perfectly proper and democratic procedure for a man to make the most of himself in ways that are sometimes not ideal from the standpoint of society. One cannot be an individual living apart from society. We all know that. There is no such thing as an individual apart from social relationships. I mean, there could not have been even a start. If we were to rear a human child absolutely stripped of every contact of a social kind, we would not have a result at the end of twenty-one years, let us say, that suggested humanity at all.

So that we have come to see that these two aspects somehow must be brought together. Then the limitations, or shall we say constraints, come on the individual as well as society. This we have always to keep in mind.

Edward Gibbon said that the triumph of barbarism was also the triumph of Christianity, by which he meant a criticism of Christianity. Toynbee, the great English historian, said that the Christian Church, founded as it was on the teaching of the prophets, laid such stress on the individual's own salvation and the development of his own character that it led to the crumbling of the Roman Empire. A pretty far-fetched conclusion, I should say, but he was trying to make clear that social concern diminished in the Roman Empire after religion began to show itself in terms of this one-sided development of the individual.

There always is a danger of that for religion. Consider mysticism. Mysticism is centered in the vision of God, the individual's vision of God. It is very easy—and this has been shown time and again in the life of the mystics—to miss the essential Christian form of religion by laying stress on the mysticism which the individual is to enjoy for himself, a vision of God, of the whole universe in God. Of course that is not a fair characterization of mysticism as a whole, but nevertheless that criticism can be passed and has been passed on mysticism.

However, we come to see the importance of the social even when we are searching for the largest and best in the individual. When we think of social contacts, necessarily we think of the vast organism that we call the state, the organization of society about which there is the closest agreement, the organization to which we all have to submit; but we have to recognize more and more, if we are going to have a free democracy, the voluntary association, small groups like churches, and civic societies. In these the exercise of social privileges and powers comes to a higher level than the exercise of those privileges and powers even in anything controlled by the state, because they are wholly voluntary. The element of force does not enter into them.

Let us look at some types of religion in their bearing on democratic procedure and the democratic way of life. I am going to mention one form, not that it is organized or systematized, or has a creed, because I do not know that it has, but it is really a form of religion, practically speaking. I refer to humanism. There is an avowed attempt on the part of a great many persons at the present time to leave all theology out of account—in the sense of any considerations beyond what we see here and now, to leave out of account all values except what we think of as strictly human values, and to take the human being and human society as the sole objects of our concern. Humanists are not a tightly cohesive organization, like the Jewish group, or like a Roman Catholic group, or a Protestant group. Nevertheless there is so much of humanism in the world that we have to take account of it because it has called forth a type of devotion which is very real.

Of course, it is easy for theologians to say that humanism, strictly speaking, with no thought of the powers back of the universe and the purpose that may be ruling them, and no thought of whether their powers are personal or not, cannot produce any high religious devotion, because the field is too limited. This overlooks the intensity of some humanists' devotion to their aims. We may say that humanism is not nourished by a deep enough source and has not a wide enough outlook, but nevertheless it is here. We may say that it wears out quickly, but in some cases it does not wear out, it goes on.

You can say that humanism is inconsistent, you can say that it is illogical, but human beings do not always go by either consistency or logic. It is a fact in the religious life of the world, this play of humanistic force and interest in men, based upon an ardor that we can think of as essentially religious.

The question would be then, of course, what influence humanism has. Well, almost all humanists think of man as the essential fact and the greatest value in the universe. Some do not. But there would necessarily be a human effect, and a social result, if we had a group of persons preaching throughout the land the worth of a human being on his own account. These prophets, if you wish to call them that, do have this on their side: that they come the nearest, I think, to putting force into the idea that a man is an end in himself.

Very often it happens that even Christian preaching conceives the soul as a soul to be redeemed, to receive the reward of eternal life, and brings in all the elements of rewards and punishments that go with theology, losing sight of the worth of the human being on his own account. It is, of course, implied in the Jewish religion and in the Christian religion, but the emphasis of the humanist is so distinctly on value in itself that it does have an immense significance in democracy which cannot be overlooked.

I do not happen to be a humanist, in the limited sense. You know that from my present position. But, as a matter of fact, I can see the worth of a type of religious effort that does keep the human being on his own account standing firmly and essentially before the attention of the world.

When we come to Judaism and Christianity, the same thing is true: these religions put great value on human beings. They have done so from the beginning, from away back before we used any such terms as "democracy" at all. The ancient Jews had the essential idea. We think sometimes, to take a significant incident, that the conflict of Elijah with the priests of Baal was primarily a religious conflict in the sense in which we ordinarily think of religion, as having to do directly with God. Well, it is that. But, when we do this we are apt to overlook the significance of the incident of Naboth's vineyard which brings out this idea of the worth of a man very, very clearly.

Of course, there is no need of my doing anything more than just remind you of the story. Queen Jezebel, the daughter of the King of Sidon, held the ideas of Israel in contempt. She believed in the worship of the Tyrian Baal, which involved human sacrifice, and an individual was nothing before him. She tried to introduce that religion into the land of which she became Queen by marrying Ahab. There was conflict with the priests of Baal, but the significance of the Naboth incident is much closer to human life. There is no miraculous element in it. It is more living than the other story.

The story is that Naboth had a vineyard that Ahab desired and Ahab was King of Israel. He was very peevish and irritable about it, and Naboth was not a very pleasant character. He was churlish. He refused a reasonable request. Ahab offered him a vineyard as good as his and offered to pay him for it—very reasonably. In modern times the vineyard would have been simply taken by the law of eminent domain.

Ahab was very decent about it, but Naboth flatly refused to yield, because he believed that he had certain rights as an Israelite, that by the customs of Israel it was absolutely his and the vineyard of his fathers, and he would not yield.

The significant thing is that in getting rid of him Queen Jezebel had to bow down to the Israelitish law. If she had had her own way, she would have made short work of it. She had to find two false witnesses who said that they heard Naboth curse God and the King, putting religion and patriotism together. She got Naboth out of the way. Then came the tremendous protest of Elijah when he met Ahab again. The Israelitish circle was not widely expanded yet, but there was in Israel that essential regard for the human being and his rights which was at least a foregleam of democracy.

One of the splendid values of the Jewish religion is its emphasis on the worth of the human being—you cannot escape it anywhere. It was in the old customs. I have in mind Wellhausen, the Old Testament scholar, who told us so unforgettably that the prophets in Israel come before the lawmakers.

This emphasis on the human is also in Christianity, which builds upon the teaching of the prophets; Jesus simply took over that teaching. Jesus did not state for the first time the double Commandment, the great, supreme Commandment. He picked out of Deuteronomy one requirement, to love God with all there is of us, heart, strength and soul. And he picked out of Leviticus another Commandment, "Thou shalt love thy neighbor as thyself." What he did was to put them together and, according to the New Testament, he added a binding clause that the second Commandment is like unto the first, and illustrated it by a wonderful parable.

Christianity, even in the Dark Ages when it preached that man was degraded, always allowed the possibility of redemption. It is not wholly fair, in talking about Christianity, to say that it has at times taught the doctrine of total depravity. That is a statement of what we see in some human lives. There are plenty of facts about human individuals that seem to suggest total depravity! We see some of it in the world at the present time, on a large scale. But, as a matter of fact, there never was a time when Christianity did not preach the possibility of redemption. No matter how degraded a man might be there was the possibility of redemption and this preaching stands out very clearly.

When we come to the ethical aspect of it the Jews were so closely knit together by their psychology, that even at the earliest time, the relation of Jew to Jew was conceived of as almost a physical tie. The Jews felt themselves so close one to another, that they almost seemed to be parts of one another. This was probably back of the old idea of a man's family having to bear the punishment for the sins of any member of it. Later on, with the greater prophets like Jeremiah and Ezekiel, there came the definite teaching of the individual covenant, but the Jews did not lose that social cohesion which has in large part made them the wonderful people they are.

Christianity has always had this in mind, more especially under the old Roman Church than under the Protestant Church until comparatively recent times. From the beginning, the Christians thought that this earth is not our abiding place and their search for a heavenly home had great influence on the way they conducted themselves in carrying on the ordinary relationships of life. Augustine's *City of God* has been studied time and time again as a political tract. He was thinking really of a heavenly city to serve as a guide for an earthly city. This makes the book a tract not in political economy but in social economy and in social organization.

So these ideas have been directly connected with these various types of religion of which I speak—humanistic, Jewish, and Roman Catholic. As you all know, at the time of the Reformation, the emphasis passed over so completely to the personal side that a great many social responsibilities were overlooked until comparatively recent times. They were overlooked formally, and yet every great church leader had his social conceptions and worked on them without saying very much about them from the religious point of view. Nevertheless, the religious point of view was implied in them.

In Martin Luther there was no very consistent conception of society. He was willing to use the force of government, without any regard to justice in the case, to put down a revolt. But in comparatively recent times, of course, there has been some change. In any community, the religious conception is held and acted on, in a degree, and at the same time other conceptions are acted on in their degree. It is a mixed-up picture.

To take an illustration from our own history, here is the Methodist Church, to which I happen to belong, dividing along a line, almost an actual physical line, between North and South, over the question of slavery. One bishop in the Southern Church held that religion must have nothing to say about social issues. That was one of the reasons why there was a separation. The Southerners complained that the Northern people kept talking about slavery. Well, they were talking on one side of it, but the other people talked just as much on the other side.

Sometimes this division, or this neglect, is not as real as you would think, but it has always been a loss when the church has refused to take account of great social issues to the extent, at least, of making some statement concerning them. I think the Protestant churches today have come at least to this: they do not think of punishing a man for any social action, I mean in the political sense, but they do insist, without attempting to control the action of individuals, that they have a right to express themselves on great social questions.

When we come, then, to look at the situation that requires consideration in our own time, the problem before us just now—of course, in this hurried sketch I cannot say all the things I would like to say—is the control of our class narrowness. Here is the danger. I spoke about voluntary organizations, but they are not necessarily voluntary; they may be racial. The selfishness that is dangerous today is not individual selfishness. All religions would unite—the humanist, the Roman Catholic, the Protestant, the Jewish—on this, that the selfish life is the wrong life, but a spirit of ardor can be developed for a class point of view, and there is a class selfishness which sets the great task at the present time, I think, before all religions alike. There is not enough widening of the field of view in terms of humanity. In spite of all we say, all our fine speeches, about human impulses and human values, we are pretty closely tied to our class when it comes to action.

We have around us divisions that follow the line of money. Here is a man who is born in the moneyed class. There are not so very many of those in America. To a certain extent it can be said still, as it was said by our fathers, "from shirt sleeves to shirt sleeves in three generations." We do not hold on to the money. But when trusteeship and trust companies came, even that tendency changed somewhat. The moneyed-class point of view begins to control almost everything.

The weakness of liberalism in the Victorian age of England was that the bases of democracy were too small. It comprised a comparatively small group, and the liberals were for democracy as long as they felt that it was beneficial to their own class. And so it has been practically everywhere else. I happen to think of a very great moneyed man—I am not mentioning any names; you may not know the name anyhow—in this country some years ago who was sent to prison, and he said the bitterest thought about it all was that the man who conducted the prosecution against him had betrayed his class. That was what hurt him. I think the man was sincere about it. He had a class consciousness.

I knew another man who was sent to prison for very irregular practices, who said, when he was let out on parole, "After all, just think, society itself now is going ahead and doing on its own account the things for which they sent me to prison." You see how he forgot the difference between himself and the state. He thought he had the right to do things for his own personal reasons, because of his standing as a member of his class, and then complained that the state was doing freely the things for which it had once condemned him.

Now you can bring pressures of a social sort to bear on an individual, but the trouble is you can so easily sanctify a class consciousness, and a man can be so unselfish, can give all the money that he has and give his body to be burned, for a class consciousness which really is socially harmful, standing as it does without any regard at all to the interests of other groups in society.

So if I were going to speak of this in terms of modern conditions, I would say that now the need is not for preaching against individual selfishness in terms of one's own relationships. That, man usually comes to hold in contempt anyhow. But it is the preaching of, and it is the standing for, a widening idea of social relationships that is needed today.

There is a place for voluntary associations, as I said a moment ago, and probably for a devotion to them greater than the mere devotion to a state as such. I mean, it may be more intense. However, just at present, there is a danger. It is in the idea of privilege. A man will say, "Yes, I have these privileges, but they came to me by providential adjustment. Why shouldn't I have them? Why shouldn't I enjoy them?" There can be a devotion to a group that really comes in the end to outright paganism, and we have to keep that danger in mind.

We must also remember this: that democracy, after all, has not reached out to the ends of the earth as yet. I do not know how soon it will, but it has not reached the ends of the earth, and there is a great deal in what Marx used to say. He used to say that human history is not yet begun, and by that he meant simply that the ordinary privileges which we think of as belonging properly and peculiarly to human life are not possible yet to the masses of mankind the world over.

One distressing fact about this whole present world crisis is this: that the conditions among the great outlying masses of humanity (that is our term: we think of ourselves as at the center when we say that and I apologize for the use of the expression) are not yet touched; that is to say, by any social measures that really bring them the conditions of human existence. Call that a missionary thought, if you wish, but that thought has to be in the mind of anybody standing for democracy, and he has to remember that as long as that situation out there is not attended to, democracy has not yet come, because you cannot talk about democracy when people have not the conditions of human living.

I do not have any practical suggestions as to how to work it out, but I do think that much more important now than to emphasize individual selfishness is to deal with this perfectly sincere, perfectly self-sacrificing devotion to classes, which, when confined to the classes themselves, is simply ruinous from the standpoint of the progress of humanity as a whole.

Let me conclude by two remarks I heard from different social students when I was a boy, which was many, many years ago. I heard one prominent social student—whose name probably would not be recognized now, though he was prominent fifty years ago—say this: that the majority of men upon the face of the earth have never at any time lain down to rest at night having known through the day the satisfaction of enough to eat. Well, that caught my imagination as a boy, and I never have forgotten it.

A little later I heard another social student, talking about religious beliefs, mention almost casually that after the study of the religious symbolisms of men he had concluded that the majority of men upon the face of the earth from the beginning of time, when they have sought to symbolize a divine being, or a divine force, have done it under some forms of dragon or serpent; very seldom have they taken a human face as the symbol. Of course, it is true that there are symbols of the latter kind, but he was speaking from the standpoint of a student of sociology concerning the whole course of human history.

I heard those two statements. Then I put the two together. You may call this the thinking of a callow youth—that used to be our favorite expression about youths—callow. I never knew what it meant. It may have been the idea of a callow youth, but I put the two things together, and came to the conclusion that the reason why the majority of men upon the face of the earth have lain down any night without having known the satisfaction of enough to eat through the day, was that men have a degraded and low conception of the universe in which they have lived.

The humanist does not do that. He makes it a universe which is a challenge to men. He says there are many things we cannot get at, but when he thinks of anything outside human life, he thinks of the glories of the discoveries of natural science. And we have all these values in our religious teaching. We have a religion—Jewish or Christian, Catholic or Protestant, as the case may be—which puts the human being up in the supreme place so far as our affairs here on earth are concerned. I think, then, that when we unite on the need of making a social organism of the right kind, we are on the path toward something that promises success, but it will be a long time before we come to any full realization of it.

The old idea of democracy was that you counted votes. Here is one, here is one, and here is one—one, two, three, four, five—the counting of the votes determines the result. That numerical conception of democracy has, of course, a political significance. But there is another conception about which we are hearing more today, and that is the organic conception, that man not only counts for one, but that man, in the scheme of things, is indispensable, so that even though his part in the social body is insignificant, nevertheless something would be lost if he were left out.

That is an essentially Jewish conception; it is an essentially Christian conception. I know this does not get very far into details, that it does not give much guidance as to any specific situation, but I do believe it suggests something of the connection between religion and democracy.

A SURVEY OF PROPOSALS FOR POSTWAR RECONSTRUCTION: A Protestant View

By

HENRY P. VAN DUSEN, D.D.

Professor of Systematic Theology, Union Theological Seminary

Amid the vast and varied plethora of schemes for postwar reconstruction which have already been forthcoming, it is not easy to discover a single principle of classification which is fully adequate and satisfactory.

I

A number of attempts have been made to sift out the agreements among these manifold proposals, and thus to frame a common platform of consensus. This effort has been directed especially toward statements by religious groups or leaders. The writer may be permitted the judgment that these efforts are of limited value. At best, they arrive at a least common denominator which tends to hide the radical divergences between the different concrete plans erected upon common general principles, and thus to disguise the extreme difficulty of securing effective agreement upon specific elements in postwar reconstruction. Their more serious weakness is that they tempt to the formulation of neat schemes constructed from a large number of blocks drawn from many quarries of varied materials and strengths—an essentially artificial and unstable construct—when it is a first requisite of any adequate scheme that it possess the resilient and flexible strength of an organism in which the detailed proposals are mutually implicit and indispensable. This tendency is one illustration of the eclecticism which is so natural but so dubious a feature of yearning in liberal circles today—the reaching out for agreements and unities to satisfy the longing for community against common enemies, in disregard of the exacting and obdurate conditions prerequisite to real and cohesive community. Here is suggested one of the major difficulties in planning for world order. It is an illustration of the familiar dilemma of the universal and the particular. What is desired is a scheme sufficiently universal to embrace interests and values as broad as humanity. What is demanded is a scheme sufficiently cohesive and resistant to hold firm amidst the titanic centrifugal and conflicting forces which dominate the world situation; therefore, a scheme with the close-knit strength of organic particularity.

II

However, almost all proposals worthy of serious consideration are agreed upon *one underlying assumption,* and also upon the specific issues which furnish *greatest difficulties* to the realization of world order. The common assumption is the *problem of power* as the dominant factor in world order, the factor which has been almost universally bypassed or underrated in idealistic thought between the Wars, the factor which must largely determine the detailed contours of any important scheme considered. The specific issues of greatest difficulty which appear in almost all discussions of world reconstruction, arranged roughly in the order in which they are likely to appear are:

1. The future of Germany—not primarily the determination of boundaries or the structure of government in the new Germany, but the deeper problem whose solution should control boundaries and government—what is to be done with the German people, the most gifted, virile and indestructible people on the Continent of Europe.
2. The location and administration of international power. This embraces the problem of police force, of world government, of armaments, and of economic arrangements (including raw materials and trade) in so far as they are vital elements in the administration of international power.

3. The status, immediate and ultimate, of subject peoples. This is the problem popularly referred to as "colonies," or "imperialism." In most, though by no means all, of the current proposals, this problem is regarded as anterior and subordinate to the problem of power.
4. The future of the Jewish people.
5. The New Order in the Far East, including the future of Japan. To some, it may seem surprising that this problem, especially the future of Japan, appears for relatively late consideration. But I believe that is the position which it holds in most informed considerations. The future of Japan is subsumed under the overarching issues of Far Eastern reordering. And both are subordinate to the more basic issue of world power and order.
6. The more distant contours of World Society—the ultimate goal to be envisioned.

III

While any too simple classification of the many plans is suspect, the two most basic considerations which determine the complex of confusing proposals and counter-proposals are, I believe, these:

a. The variant views of the fashion in which international power should be located and administered.
b. Divergence as to whether postwar arrangements should be an organic development of prewar practice, or whether what is demanded is a "New Deal" in international affairs—quite new principles and procedures in world organization.

Of these two considerations, the second is less widely recognized but is, I believe, the more fundamental and determinative. In illustrating its outworkings, we shall draw largely upon thought in Great Britain and the United States, partly because thought in those two countries has been more fully articulated and is more readily accessible; partly because presumably Britain and America will, in fact, wield a larger influence in the ultimate determinations than any other nation or combination of nations; partly because it would be expected that agreement might be more easily achieved between the ruling elements in these two countries than elsewhere, and if achieved such agreement might wield a quite determinative force in world decisions, while if agreement between Great Britain and the United States is not possible, the realization of a wider consensus to embrace all those charged with decision making appears wellnigh chimerical.

I say, divergence as to whether postwar arrangements should move in continuity with prewar practice or should proceed upon quite new principles marks the central dividing line among postwar planners. The disputants favor respectively organic development and a New Deal in world politics. In general, this is also the line of cleavage between best informed and most responsible opinion in the two great English-speaking peoples.

But within each camp, there are two clearly distinguishable viewpoints, the more moderate and the more extreme, differentiated by the rigor with which the controlling principle of continuity or novelty is applied. Thus we face, in fact, not two but four main positions.

At one extreme are those, usually traditionalist in temperament, disillusioned or cynical as to the possibility of the control of world affairs by reason or abstract justice, who believe with greater or less frankness in the philosophy of *real politik*. They are disposed to hark back to the nineteenth century as the great century of the Modern Era; to point to the relative stability maintained throughout that century through the instrumentality of the balance of power and the so-called *Pax Brittanica;* to locate the Modern World's deviation from the path of sound advance at Versailles' departures from tried and established principles of international statecraft under the persuasion of Utopian idealists; to lodge major blame for today's holocaust upon the weakness and impracticability of the League of Nations, and to seek a return to nineteenth century patterns properly revised and adapted to the present state of world life. In brief, the return to the *status quo ante*—not ante World War II, but ante World War I. Those who hold this view are likely to advocate severe measures upon Germany assuring her emasculation if not dismemberment, the eschewing of world economic or political organization, the continuance essentially unmodified of traditional colonial policies and status, the fostering of a new Asiatic balance of power with a weak China and a chastened but reconstituted Japan held in balance under the aegis of a benevolent Anglo-American sponsorship.

In Britain, this general viewpoint is given most extreme advocacy by Sir Robert Vansittart and his colleagues. But let us not fall into the error of labeling it a distinctively "British viewpoint." While detailed proposals would vary, this has been the underlying mentality reflected in the dominant philosophy of American foreign policy throughout most of the past hundred years. Its presuppositions were those of Senator Lodge and his colleagues in 1920. On the whole, it has ruled the councils of the Republican Party since. The evidence is by no means unambiguous that its grip upon the underlying assumptions of the directors of that party has been shaken, except in the case of Mr. Willkie and a few others whose leadership within party circles is, at best, dubious. Moreover, it is far more than a party mentality. This *is* the underlying mentality of large masses of the American people. No one who studies the illogical movements of mass psychology should need persuasion that it remains as a powerful latent substratum within the American mind. Since its own governing principle is reliance upon the *status quo,* it tends to claim the instinctive allegiance of all typical Americans just because it represents our own traditional habit-patterns of both thought and practice.

At the opposite extreme are those who seem to all three alternative groups to have learned nothing from the tragedies of the past twenty years. At least, they have been led to no fundamental change in their comprehension of the problem of power and their proposals for handling it. They believe that our international ills stem directly from the mismanagement of bigoted and selfish statesmen, and that the first and principal requirement for the cure of those ills is the displacement of traditional leadership and the radical replacement of habitual presuppositions and practices of statecraft by a "New Order." This viewpoint is so familiar to those whose associations are with religious groups in this country that it demands no detailed exposition, for it is precisely within these American groups that it finds its most fertile breeding-ground. Its appeal is to reason and sweet reasonableness. Its reliance is upon the inherent goodness and good sense of the "common man." The governing device of its strategy is to assure that the will of the common people shall achieve fulfillment in the decisions of governments. Its proposals for the difficult specific decisions in world reordering are also familiar—peace through negotiation at the earliest possible moment with representative and trusted leaders of the German and Japanese people, then the encouragement of democratic institutions within Germany and the immediate restoration of the German nation to full power and fellowship within the community of nations; the immediate and full emancipation of all subject peoples, beginning with India today; complete and universal disarmament; the creation of a new World Society functioning through a World Government constituted by representatives of all peoples of the world and operating by constitutional legislative, judicial and executive procedures with minimal police provisions and powers. In brief, world reordering should take its start from the ultimate goal of World Society and all specific arrangements should be deduced as corollaries.

I shall make no attempt to appraise either the validity or value of this position. If criticisms are to be raised with regard to it, they cannot be directed toward its sincerity or toward its lofty and appealing ideal. They must challenge the adequacy of its comprehension of the world scene. Indeed, ultimately, they must challenge the adequacy of its comprehension of human nature whose relationships constitute the realities of world problems. Its critics will also doubtless point out that, by a logic which is familiar in human affairs, this position, if disillusioned as to the fulfillment of its plans, often tends to retreat into despair as to the possibility of world order on any other basis—and therefore to take refuge in an isolationism closely akin to that of Position 1. Precisely this was the logically contradictory but psychologically understandable alliance of many traditionalists and disillusioned idealists in the United States between 1921 and 1941.

IV

There remain the two intermediate and more moderate positions, differentiated less in their conceptions of the ultimate goals of world order than in their view of the manner in which and speed with which those goals should be sought. One favors a gradual and progressive approach to the many complicated issues of world peace and world organization, the generous employment of experimentation, but the eschewing of predetermined blueprints and sudden and radical change. The other sees little hope for significant results except through drastic change, distrusts the arrangements and instruments of the era which has precipitated two world conflicts in a quarter century, welcomes the opportunity which the flux of war offers for new structures and radical changes in political order.

The first is disposed to reason that the method of sudden change in deference to an abstract scheme of ideal principles had its trial in the post-Versailles arrangements, especially the League of Nations, and failed. The precipitation of the present conflict is interpreted largely as a direct and inevitable outcome of this well-intentioned but unsound method of international reconstruction, which neglects, it is held, the essentially organic character of sound social institutions, the profound rootage of traditional loyalties, the impossibility of bending the habits of history and natural affinity to some ideal but abstract pattern. The second argues that the post-Versailles arrangements centering in the League failed not because they were unsound but because they were never given fair trial, not because too much was expected of them but because too little authority was entrusted to them to enable a demonstration of their soundness. It points to the sudden and radical reordering following all revolutionary cataclysms—notably the French, American and Russian revolutions—as proof of the malleability of social institutions and the salutary outcome of drastic change. It points to our experimental and unsatisfactory trial period under the Confederation, leading, not to scrapping of the principle of Federalism, but to its strengthening under the Constitution. It believes that the way of advance lies, not in rejecting the inter-war experience and returning to the tested and familiar (but, as it would hold, discredited) procedures of nineteenth century statecraft, but in a fearless resumption of the recent pattern, revised and greatly strengthened from the lessons of its first trial.

The first position favors the assumption of responsibility for post-war peace and order by the Four Great Powers among the United Nations, with the collaboration of their associates, but with predominant influence probably resting in Great Britain and the United States. The second envisions a reconstituted association of nations embracing at once all non-Axis Powers and welcoming the defeated nations at the earliest practicable hour, an association of nations differing from the League not only in certain details of organization, but in the more vital strengthening of its authority by the imposition of real though sharply defined limitations upon irresponsible freedom of national action and the lodgment of adequate police power in the central authority. I have suggested that here lies the line of cleavage between the best informed and most trustworthy opinion in the two great English-speaking partners. Since so much hangs on the achievement of fuller understanding and, if possible, agreement between Great Britain and the United States, it is worth while to explore the grounds of this deviation somewhat fully.

The differences in characteristic British and American viewpoints regarding political reordering are due partly to contrasts in national temperament. In part, they very largely reflect contrasted experiences with government, both their own governments and rule over subject peoples, which, in turn, may be caused by or may be the causes of the more subtle differences which we speak of as temperamental. Behind these differences in political experience, again, lie more fundamental differences in the understanding of man, and of the fashion in which, because of man's nature, government should be ordered.

Quite naturally, each nation tends to project upon the world scene that type of procedure and structure which has worked most satisfactorily in its own history, and with which in consequence it feels most confidently at home. The British constitutional system, with the empire it governs, has grown like Topsy. Hence the British aversion to blueprints and written instruments of government. But America's experience has been under a written constitution. Americans believe it has worked satisfactorily. They are disposed to assume it as providing an appropriate precedent for world government.

By the same token, the characteristic British method of advance is trial and error, often defined, not without pride, as "muddling through." It speaks out of an experience of centuries rather than decades, marked by few drastic changes but by steady experimental growth. And it speaks out of experience in government across the earth and over many peoples. Hence the British aversion to the radically different and the drastically new. Their natural conceptions are organic, developmental. On the other hand, the American people speak out of political knowledge to be measured in decades, from the perspective of a nation born fullgrown in revolution, and from experience confined almost entirely to a homogeneous people within one continent. To the British misgiving of sudden change, they point to their own history in answer. To the British emphasis upon organic development rather than forced conformity to abstract principles, however admirable, they cite their own Constitutional experience as adequate proof. Hence the American receptivity to revolutionary change, the American confidence in fresh experiments.

Again, with regard to the possibilities for self-government by backward peoples, Britain's unique success in administration has been achieved within the structure of an Empire under the ideal of stewardship, supported somewhat covertly by the stratagem of "divide and rule" through the manipulation of the balance of power. The British believe that influence and responsibility should be directly proportional to effective power. Those nations upon which will fall, in the last analysis, responsibility for preserving world peace should be directly charged with responsibility and direction of world government. The view of human nature implicit in the American view, though seldom made explicit or even recognized by most Americans, is more pessimistic as regards the strong, more hopeful as regards the backward. Fated by geography to be a great power, many Americans still retain an ingrained suspicion of massed power. Destined in spite of themselves to be an empire, they are still averse to empires and empire building. Conversely, they are quick in sympathy for small or ill-favored peoples, having so recently emerged from a very modest beginning by an industry which has hewn a continental empire out of intractable circumstance. We are disposed to favor education of the backward in responsibility. On the other hand, our authentic American tradition harbors a deep distrust of the wielders of great power. We recognize the tendency of might toward domination. Our system of government is founded upon the principle of tethering power by checks and balances. We are far less uncomfortable if influence is granted to small nations disproportionate to their real strength.

These differences in national presupposition and viewpoint are not new. They came to expression no less sharply in the last postwar settlement than at the present time. On the whole, the specific provisions of the Versailles Treaty followed the British pattern more closely than ours. But the League of Nations was America's contribution to the peace. It was a characteristically American device—in its proposal to create world government *de novo,* in its grounding of that government upon abstract principles of justice and equity, and even in the details of its structural arrangements. In principle, the structure of the League was a closely parallel reproduction of the American constitutional system—two legislative houses; the upper house representing the larger centers of power; but its actions checked by a lower house, equally representative of all nations, large or small. In the Assembly of the League, there was a deliberate defiance of the principle, so clearly indicated by logic and axiomatic to British constitutional minds, that influence should be directly proportional to responsibility, and that those upon whom rests the task of enforcing international order should have preponderant voice in determining the character of that order.

Enthusiasm for the League was always warmer in this country than in Great Britain, though never strong enough to bring the

American people to assume the slightest responsibility for the child of their devising and creation. Europe had the actual experience of wrestling with the League in all its inadequacies and ultimate futilities. It cannot be too strongly stressed that in Europe in general, and in Britain in particular, disillusionment with the whole League idea and pattern is far deeper than among idealists in this country. Most American internationalists were profoundly committed to the principles of the League. Disillusioned as they were over its comparative ineffectiveness, they attribute its "failure" first of all to American abstention, and then to manipulation of the League in the interests of the Great Powers. Their faith in the fundamental soundness of the "League idea" is unshaken. As already suggested, they hold scant hope for enduring peace save through return to the plan of a world association, revised toward strength.

This deviation appears very sharply in typical British and American attitudes toward the problem of colonies. A characteristic American viewpoint, frankly expressed not only by idealists but by political realists of high influence within and beyond government circles, is that the era of Imperialism is gone forever. The implication, often made explicit, is that all colonial peoples should be immediately liberated; if any vestige of foreign supervision continues, it should be through international supervision or administration. This general intention, it is held, should be given concrete manifestation in the immediate liberation of India. The most enlightened British view, when frankly expressed is likely to run somewhat as follows: "We fully agree that the era of Imperialism is past. We fully share your desire and intention that all presently subject peoples shall be encouraged and aided to go forward to full self-government at the fastest practicable pace. But we query the wisdom of your specific proposals at two points. First, such sudden and drastic disruption of institutions and structures painstakingly developed over a century or more will wreak catastrophic and disastrous effects upon the welfare of these peoples. You are destroying an organism for the immediate forms of independence. All true advance is through organic development, not sudden revolution. Second, it does not seem to occur to you that backward peoples, if they must continue to have a measure of supervision and outside assistance, may prefer the continuance of their present mentors rather than sudden subjection to utter strangers, especially the dubious device of an international authority."

These two views have been analyzed and illustrated as though they were representative of British and American opinion respectively. Any such presentation, if left without further comment, would be seriously misleading. And, in two respects. First, while the "gradualist" philosophy is more typically British than American, it also controls the thinking of large numbers of the best informed and most influential students of the world scene in this country. Indeed, there is some reason to think that it may represent the underlying philosophy of those who now speak officially for the American nation and are likely to be their spokesmen in the peace making. Second and much more important, we have spoken as though gradualism were the British philosophy, the New Deal that of the United States. But we have been speaking solely of political reordering. The most significant paradox in the present situation is that in Britain it is universally assumed that we are going forward to radical reordering of economic and social life, while there is a preference for slow and careful readjustments in international arrangements. In this country, there is a cry for a New Order internationally, but in the matter of domestic economy, the forces of reaction—of return to the *status quo ante*—have already powerfully set in. In brief, each nation desires radical change where it has no present interest at stake or where its own interests counsel such change; each nation favors gradualism if not stagnation where its own interests appear imperiled. If this be a distressing, a disillusioning (some would suggest, a cynical) observation, it is best that we face it. It leads to this tragic generalization concerning the policies of nations—no nation is willing to advocate idealistic solutions which appear to cut across its own national interests. Conversely, nations will lend their support to right solutions, however clearly they may be indicated by the logic of events and the warnings of contemporary history, *only* if their own interests justify their support, or at least, if no great threat to national self-interest is involved.

V

Thus we are brought to a final observation. If I may be permitted to repeat words written a year ago which seem to me no less true today: "In the making of peace, the significant divisions will not be, as will be made to appear, between victors and vanquished, or even between nations allied in victory. The real divisions will be *within* nations, within each nation. . . . The great necessity is that those who so envision the peace and are committed to its realization should discern clearly where our real problem lies—not between nations but within each nation; that we should acknowledge that the bonds uniting like-purposed people of every nation are more intimate and more commanding of allegiance than those which join us with fellow-countrymen; that we should have thought our way through to a common mind as to the peace we seek; and then that we should struggle shoulder to shoulder within our respective nations for the actual achievement of the common goals lest mankind's hopes again suffer shipwreck."

A SURVEY OF PROPOSALS FOR POSTWAR RECONSTRUCTION: A Catholic View

By

JOHN LaFARGE, S.J., B.A.

Associate Editor, "America"

I remember reading of a small boy who disliked big events, because events make history, and he hated history. For such a small boy, the first three weeks of November, 1942, must have been unusually trying. They have been crowded with events, and history is being made faster than we can talk about it. The elections have brought us a vivid sense of the trends in our own country, for better or for worse, according to our respective points of view. They have shown, anyhow, that we are, contrary to many doleful predictions, still able to register our own opinions whether or not these are pleasing to the government in power.

Mr. Willkie's tour of the world directed our minds and our comment to the thought of millions upon the other side of the globe. With the invasion of North Africa and our victories in the Solomons the war takes a new turn, and we see dimly ahead of us further turns that will in time bring us to the end of the long road.

At the same time, we find upon our doorstep a whole basketful of political problems. We avoid them and prudently disclaim concern about them. We shall let the people of France work out their differences in their own way, since there is no occupation less profitable than that of directing Frenchmen how to adjust their own affairs. We assure the divided people of India that we shall clear out promptly when the fighting is over, and we shall not try to harmonize India's Congress and Britain's Sir Stafford and Mr. Amery by any guidance from Washington. But none the less our eyes begin to turn more anxiously than before to the political and social struggles of the future era.

In the dim distance, we see approaching the day when we shall be obliged to make a fateful decision between the many plans for the structure of the postwar world that now are laid daily upon our desks for our consideration. Every one of us receives them. They come in books, in booklets and pamphlets, in magazine articles, in deliberations of societies, committees, seminars and various institutions. They are intelligent and unintelligent: inspiring and depressing; disinterested and highly self-seeking; they are universal in their point of view, or they are narrow and nationalistic. They are devoted to saving all that is possible of the old world, for fear of a much worse state of things if we depart from the sound lessons of the past. Or they are for sweeping revolutions, taking the opportunity now or never to rebuild the world according to their desire.

If we consider some of the principal fields in which decisions will have to be made—about which decisions are already being made—we cannot help asking ourselves: What part will religion play in the formation of such decisions?

The decision must be made whether or not we are to recognize the existence of God, in our public as well as in our private lives, and recognize the sacredness of His immutable laws. Will we finally come to realize that without God there can be no lasting peace or firmly established political or social order?

We shall be obliged to reach a decision about the position, in the new scheme of things, of the family; whether or not it is to be restored to its position of primacy, all the more necessary because of the tremendous dislocation and disruption the family is suffering in the war. This applies in full measure to our own country, where evil influences are destroying the family.

We must be able to make up our minds once and for all whether or not we are to live in amity with the other peoples of the world; whether there shall be not only amity, but a solid and constructive unity, between the different racial, national and religious groups in our community; and whether this principle is to apply to the entire world. We cannot continue to vacillate as we now are doing, blowing hot and cold, first one way then another.

We cannot expect, for instance, to adopt a policy of amity for all the most distant peoples of the world, to expect them to love us and to love one another and to compose their various differences, and lay down here at home absolutes, founded upon pure emotion and hereditary custom, which we ourselves can never relinquish.

We cannot expect to construct a lasting international order unless there is some agreement as to a code of international law. The decision confronts us as to whether we can operate a world society without such a code of law; and if not, then what shall be its nature? If we agree upon a code of law, we are confronted likewise with the problem of decisions as to the juridical institutions which will interpret, embody and enforce or administer that law. What shall we decide upon as a means of enforcing and guaranteeing the faithful fulfilment of the peace terms, and preventing arbitrary breaches and unilateral interpretations of treaties?

A decision must be reached as to the fundamental, natural rights of states, such as the enjoyment of liberty, political and territorial integrity and security. Shall we come definitely to the conclusion, once and for all, that the true liberty of a state exists not only in the affirmation of autonomy and sovereign rule, but also in the acknowledgment of such autonomy in accordance with the natural law?

What answers shall be finally given to the questions of national or racial minorities? Shall we accept the dictum of Pope Pius XII, that within the limits of a new order, "there is no place for open or secret oppression of the cultural and linguistic characteristics of national minorities"?

As for the decisions to be made in the economic sphere, religion must necessarily have its say, for if there is one outstanding lesson of the present world situation, it is that economic questions cannot be decided by economics alone. All these many questions: access to raw materials, trade and tariff barriers, differences and harmonizations in national and international standards of living, public works and employment, matters that already arouse such anxious speculation and such bitter debate—all these are affected ultimately by the individual's view as to the real meaning of life, the destiny of the earthly goods with which the Creator has endowed man. And these, in the long run, resolve themselves into the question of religion.

It is impossible, therefore, to omit from our consideration the question of the place of religion itself in the postwar order. It is not enough to ask: Will religion be honored or will it be persecuted? This question is important enough. Obviously, there can be no amity, freedom, peace or order in the world, if any person or group of persons are to be the object of attack by the state, or by any section within it, because of religious convictions sincerely held. An even more fundamental question confronts us: Will religion be allotted the place that it claims for itself, of being the expression and interpretation in the lives of men of the ultimate reality of the universe?

In putting the matter that way, I am pointing to a decision which needs to be made by all religious-minded men now, at the present moment, not to be relegated to the uncertain future. Evidently, as religious-minded men and women, we are anxious to see that religion is accorded an honored place in the coming scheme of things, and so, by its presence, it will be in a position to influence those many decisions a few of which I have briefly indicated.

But merely to plan, in a sort of general way, for an honored place for religion is not enough. We need, it seems to me, to make up our minds whether or not we are to work merely for the toleration of religion, or are we to insist that religion be accorded its proper place as the authority upon the ultimate realities of human existence.

Are we to work for a minimum or for a maximum program, in this respect?

When I speak of religion as the authority upon the ultimate reality of man's existence, I am speaking of a religion which places that ultimate reality in something which is above and beyond man: a religion, in other words, which looks to God as the source of man's being, and the final goal of his existence. Such a religion finds the full interpretation of the finite only in terms of the Infinite; finds the ultimate basis of the dignity and authority of the human person in the unchanging dignity of a Divine Personality.

The question is far from academic, as to whether or not we shall maintain or obtain the position of religion that I have just indicated. Such a position is already fiercely disputed. Undoubtedly, it will be still more fiercely disputed in the future. There are many claimants to the throne of the interpreter of the ultimate reality. The unfortunate thing is the misfortune that has so often attended controversies of this sort in the past: that the attempt to vindicate religion's rightful place, over the claims of physical or social science, of psychology, or history, or any other branch of human knowledge or activity, is apt to take the form of depreciation of these same branches of human knowledge. The religionist, in disputing some physicists' claim to say the last word about the realities of the world and man's position in it, is apt to appear in the highly unwelcome and thoroughly false light of an enemy of science, a foe to progress, and obscurantist zealot, etc. In some cases he may actually deserve such a term of reproach, but he need not be in that position.

In the propounding of such a question, I may be met by the objection: if you lay such supreme stress upon religion, if you make religion the court of last resort for those things that rightfully go to the court of last resort, are you not making all human agreement really impossible? For there is no prospect of any immediate agreement as to the dictates of religion. Religion deals with ultimates. But no disagreements are more intense than those which deal with ultimates. Many anxious persons are so moved by this consideration that they consider it wiser and safer to keep religion in a subordinate or second place, so that people may battle about less essential matters, but not come to the calamity of a religious warfare.

My answer to that, however, is that the dangers of religious conflict, in a violent and inhuman form, are far greater when religion is placed in a subordinate position to human passions and extraneous interests, than when it is given its rightful place in human society. I believe we shall see our way much clearer in planning for the postwar world, if we frankly recognize the fact that a great number of our citizens have no concept that there is or can be any ultimate reality by which decisions are to be taken in the field of wider human relationships. They are moved by their inherited sentiments, by their immediate impressions and the resultant emotions.

The condition we are facing cannot be met by arousing counter emotions; nor can it be dealt with by mere reasoning. I believe that the simplest and most direct way for religion to obtain its rightful position in forming the decisions of the postwar world, is for religion to assert its rightful position; to assert its position plainly, consistently, and repeatedly, on every available occasion.

Few will deny, I think, that the modern mind is greatly influenced by repeated assertion. This may not be a desirable state of affairs, but it is apparent on every side. It is apparent in the case of religion. The warfare against religion in modern times has been conducted, in great measure, not by a process of reasoning, but largely by mere assertion. "Religion is the opium of the people." "Religion is the death of the soul." Religion, that is to say, a spiritual, transcendent and theistic religion, is a traitor to blood and soil. "Religion is a purely private affair, and should not meddle in the affairs of state, of society, of economics," etc. "It is purely relative, a matter of custom, emotion or tradition."

These bald assertions have had their effect in working confusion in the modern mind. It would be a shallow philosophy to be satisfied with a mere countering of assertions. Nevertheless, I believe there is a definite function for the simple assertion of the truth, when it is face to face with the audacity of error. Let me ask you, therefore, if now is not the time when such a simple but repeated assertion is particularly needed.

Heavy as is the challenge of the present moment to religion, it is likewise religion's opportunity. The circumstance that the visible order of things is undergoing violent change offers all the greater occasion to point out that none of the phenomena of change and becoming can be seen in their true perspective, none can be adequately understood, save in the light of the invisible, unchanging Being who guides the destinies of the world.

I believe that the President's appointment of Governor Lehman, as director of the work of rehabilitation in the liberated countries, will give the specific opportunity for the type of assertion which I have had in mind.

My first ground for this belief is the record which Governor Lehman has already established in the assertion of religious principle. If I may quote from the address that the Governor gave in this very institution a fortnight ago (November 8, 1942):

> "The task which devolves upon us is . . . threefold: first, to defeat the men of arrogance who are today struggling with military might to enslave the world; second, so to convince ourselves of the value of the moral and spiritual truths that they will become guides to our conduct in private and public life; and third, through precept and example to win the world to a recognition of the moral principles involved in these teachings.
>
> "This, it seems to me, is a task in the purview of the religious teachers of our time. They can bring to mankind a recognition of the supreme value of the human personality, and a universal desire to serve and know God. With these principles established and adopted, efforts to enslave mankind, to use men as tools, to deny them the equal dignity bestowed on all as the children and the servants of the living God, would become impossible.
>
> "Our democratic traditions are the offspring of the great religious teachings of past generations. . . . The ideas which guided Thomas Jefferson in writing the Declaration of Independence, can be traced back through the heritage of the Puritan evangelist, the Catholic philosopher, the Mohammedan sage and the Jewish rabbi to the fountainheads of all western religion—the sacred Scriptures. The history of the past two decades has shown that the religious traditions are not merely the channels through which democratic ideas have come to us, but in the last analysis, the means by which these ideas must be preserved and expanded. . . .
>
> "Without venturing into theology, I believe we can all recognize the guiding hand of Providence even in the appalling events of our time."

"We give aid and comfort to the enemies of democracy," said the Governor in the series of points that he laid down as a summary of the relation between religious principles and democratic ideals, "when we encourage anti-religious or pagan teachings which undermine the foundations of democracy."

My second ground for this belief is the type of work that the Governor has been appointed to engage in. This vast work of rehabilitation necessarily brings those who engage in it into direct contact with the ultimate realities of man's existence. To be effective, it must appeal to man's highest motives, to his charity, patience, unselfishness and self-sacrifice, to his sense of honor and justice. Those who are occupied therein will be obliged to deal with movements and agencies, in the social and political world, which will endeavor to use the work of rehabilitation for their own ends, and to lay therein the seeds of future dissensions and even future wars.

An appeal will be constantly made to realities, but few men have the faith and courage to rise to the thought of the ultimate realities. It is never pleasant to think too long or too consistently upon what is ultimately real. Such thought is a strain on one's patience. It is, furthermore, a severe strain on man's vanity and innate pride. The more we learn of the greatness of God, the vastness of His scheme of things, the wonders of His providence and the mystery of His guidance, the greater the claim on our store of humility, and for most of us, humility from birth has been quite considerably rationed. We can parcel it out in small allotments, on occasion, but few of us dare dispense it too generously, for fear we may see ourselves too plainly as we are.

Yet in that unrationed humility is the hope of a new world. Not the humility of a self-depreciation inspired, in fact, by cowardice and a secret pride. But the humility which springs from wisdom, which has the courage to look beyond the passing scene to the eternity from which man comes and unto which he will return.

It is the dread of that humility, of its stark realism, which, at bottom, is the source of the fear entertained by so many lest religion assert itself too boldly. If any task requires such humility, it is certainly the task of trying to bring order into the torment of the liberated nations after the war. If we Americans approach that task in any other spirit, our pride and our conceit will immediately betray us, and we shall sooner or later find our best efforts frustrated. I can think of no stronger guarantee, on the other hand, for success in this work, than for America to come forth, as I assume it is the Governor's intention it shall come forth, as the definite asserter of religious validity, religious freedom and religious relevancy to the new social order, in the reconstruction of the world.

A SURVEY OF PROPOSALS FOR POSTWAR RECONSTRUCTION: A Jewish View

By

BEN ZION BOKSER, Ph.D.

Rabbi, Forest Hills Jewish Center

I

Postwar reconstruction involves many varied tasks. It involves political reorganization, economic and cultural renewal, and above all, the reclamation of human beings from a thousand hurts and fears that a tragic ordeal will have imposed on them. But if the new peace is to be more than another armistice, to be followed before long by a fresh outbreak of violence, we must also reexamine the postulates on which we have heretofore based the edifice of our civilization.

It is customary, in religious pronouncements, to trace the collapse of civilization to a decline in religious values, to a waning faith in God. Thus the Reverend James M. Gillis tells us that "the cause behind the cause of Nazism and Communism and of all the evils that flow from those two poisoned sources is atheism. The cure is to bring back God, the ultimate absolute Truth, Justice and Right. Do that and you shall have a basis upon which to reconstruct even this tottering civilization" (*Current Religious Thought,* December, 1941).

In a certain context of ideas, such a statement conveys a definite truth. Without a delineation of the idea context, however, it is meaningless. It is, for instance, possible to conceive God erroneously and nothing is more fatal for the world than to build its structures of human relations on a false view of God. Indeed, certain religious convictions have been among the basic postulates on which we have built our now tottering civilization. Religion, therefore, cannot regard itself as wholly outside the world collapse. It has been in it, and the reexamination of postulates must reach to all areas of our culture, the religious as well as the secular.

II

It was the prophet Micah who stated the point of departure for the revaluation of values with which we must meet any crisis in civilization: "The Lord's voice crieth unto the city. . . . Hear ye the rod and who hath appointed it" (Micah 6:9). To heed the moral of the rod and to know the source by which it was appointed is the crux of our problem. It is, if you will, another phase of that most baffling of all problems, the problem of what we call evil. Where man's greatest prize lies, there also lies his greatest failure. There is no more precious truth and no more fatal error than in the realm where we react to the challenge of the rod.

From the standpoint of Judaism, all experience, what we call good and what we call evil, flows alike from the same creative source, a beneficent and provident God. Evil is the by-product of sin, whether of commission or omission, while man's capacity to sin is an inevitable concomitant of his free will. But life is not destined to be a permanent comedy of errors, for God is forever prodding man to use his freedom in ever more righteous decisions. Through vision and suffering man is learning and growing; and the theme of that learning and growth is an integration of the various particularities of life in a pattern of universal harmony. History is the unfolding of this great and epic theme. It is the realm where men register their progress, their triumphs and failures in the climb upward; and every decision in history contributes to advancing or retarding man from his goal. What we call evil thus ceases to be evil, for it is a step in the direction of the good. It is the bitterness of the medicine by which we are being healed.

III

The antithesis of this monotheistic interpretation of life is dualism in various forms; and most of the failures of our world may be traced to actions and value judgments in which is enmeshed the dualistic heresy.

In its most primitive form we meet this heresy in our secular culture. Some people regard life as a series of disparate and unrelated experiences, some of which contribute to their comfort while others do not. But they see no higher law that includes them. Concealed in a variety of trappings, this view is present in national isolationism, in so far as isolationism involves an anarchic view of history in which it is held possible for nations to escape the consequences of evil by withdrawing into a private reservation, where it will not reach them. From the standpoint of monotheistic religion, all life is woven together into an organic whole; all particularities are included in a universal context of being. And ultimate isolationism is impossible just as it is impossible for a particular organ in the body permanently to shelter itself from the fate that befalls other individual organs or the collective life of the body as a whole. This anarchic view is a blind alley from the standpoint of reconstruction; for if we treat catastrophe as a chance eruption, we shall not feel impelled to mend the breaches.

IV

A more sophisticated version of this heresy, also in secular culture, is the division of mankind into distinct categories of good and evil. Certain members of the human race are credited with being creative, and others with being destructive. That leads to the dangerous though simple illusion that all you have to do is exterminate the group that is destructive, and a great peace will settle upon the world. In Germany the doctrine is taught that the Nordic race alone is creative; while the Jews are the source of evil. There are some who have paid the Nazis the compliment of mimicry; following Hitler's tribalism, they identify the German people with the principle of evil. Others trace it to Japan. What is characteristic in these attitudes is that the aggression of which the Axis nations are the present carriers is regarded as inherent in the racial strain of the German or the Japanese people. And the kind of peace settlement toward which this conception points is a settlement by vindictiveness.

From the standpoint of a monotheistic religion, there cannot be any inherently evil races, since all men are the children of God and God would not make anything that is inherently evil. As the rabbis teach us, the Biblical doctrine that all mankind is derived from a single person dramatizes the basic equality of all human beings; they are all endowed with the same capacities for vice and for virtue (Sanhedrin 38a; Tosefta Sanhedrin 8:4). Germany and Japan, too, belong to the human family. They are also endowed with unique resources of wisdom and of life that, properly channeled, can be a means of serving the world. The process of redemption must reach them also and, after a purging that will hurt mightily, but also heal, these gifted nations will take their legitimate places in the human community. As Eduard Heimann puts it: "To underestimate the German crime would make us accomplices . . . To preach forgiveness as a political solution would seem ridiculous. Yet revenge is not peace and must not be tolerated in the peace" ("Problems in European Reorganization," in *Christianity and Crisis,* May 18, 1942, p. 6).

The renunciation of vindictiveness does not mean a renunciation of the principle of retribution. "Charity to a sinner," taught Maimonides, "is cruelty to all creatures" (Guide, III, ch. 39). It is ultimately no less cruel to the sinner, for it will obscure from him the frightfulness of his deed and retard the process of his purging. The one hope for the reclamation of the aggressor nations and, for that matter, of the world, is in the rod, in which there is, to be sure, suffering but in which, as the Psalmist affirmed, there is also comfort (Psalm 23:4).

Thoughtful Germans are in accord with this position. Thus Mr. Heimann in the article cited offers this significant observation: "The main character-forming event in Germany was probably the Reformation, which taught Germany the ethic of an unconditional surrender of the individual to the state, whose power, however selfish, was meant to check the disruptive egoism of individuals and groups. This doctrine made even the bourgeoisie in Germany immune to liberalism and democracy. The Germans may dislike the Nazis, but they obey them by virtue of their innate reverence for the powers of the state. If the most concentrated form of that power is decisively beaten and its ruinous character revealed, as did not happen at the end of the First World War, then at last there is a reasonable hope that Germany may revert to more liberal ideas of government."

I am not altogether in a position to judge Mr. Heimann's appraisal of the Reformation, but his conclusion is significant. Indeed, under the impact of this doctrine many students of international affairs have come to revise their judgment of the peace by which we closed the First World War. Thus Dr. Ernest Martin Hopkins, President of Dartmouth College, declared at the recent Herald Tribune Forum, "It was an unreal humanitarianism that allowed the First World War to end at the German boundary." He continued with the warning: "Until the so-called educational system of Germany is thrown into reverse and a new generation has been compelled to distinguish between the search for truth and officially prescribed falsehood, she should not again be given the privilege of self-determination as to educational method" (*New York Herald Tribune Forum Supplement,* November 22, 1942).

The administration of justice on an international scale is surely no less hazardous than the administration of justice within a particular social order. However, it becomes justice and within the realm of ethical behavior when it aims not to destroy but to rehabilitate. As Queen Wilhelmina declared: "The thirst for revenge will be great and understandable. Let us not, however, let revenge be our guiding motive. Revenge is barren, except in that it breeds revenge. Let justice be our aim, justice and firmness tempered by wisdom." Perhaps the most hopeful promise of a peace without vindictiveness is the declaration of the Atlantic Charter which promises "to further the enjoyment by all states, great or small, victor or vanquished, of access on equal terms, to the trade and the raw materials of the world which are needed for their economic prosperity."

V

Marxism has popularized another variety of dualism. The root of evil is traced to a particular social class, the capitalists. They are the makers of war and of every variety of tyranny in the world. Labor alone is guiltless and stands outside the sins of our society. The deduction that follows from this class tribalism is that you merely liquidate the class that incarnates sin and the redemption will be at hand.

All the energy that communism can command is today pitted in the struggle against the aggressor nations; and the Soviet Union has written magnificent chapters in the epic of resistance to Hitlerism. But for the sake of historical clarity and, above all, for the sake of the new thinking that must be done as a prelude to a durable peace, we must not ignore the destructive role that Marxism has played in the unfolding of the current world tragedy.

One of the corollaries that Marxist theoreticians have drawn from their class analysis of society is the classic indictment of the state. No matter what its form, till the proletariat holds undisputed control over it, the state is always the great enemy. The state, in the words of Engels, is always "the state of the most powerful economic class that by force of its economic supremacy becomes also the ruling political class, and thus acquires new means of subduing and exploiting the oppressed masses. The ancient state was, therefore, the state of the slave owners for the purpose of holding the slaves in check. The feudal state was the organ of the nobility for the oppression of the serfs and dependent farmers. The modern representative (democratic) state is the tool of the capitalist exploiters of wage labor" (quoted by V. I. Lenin, *The Teachings of Karl Marx,* N.Y., 1933, p. 31).

The classic line of Marxist politics, therefore, became a relentless struggle for the weakening of the liberal democratic state, a struggle that continued even when the menace of fascism loomed on the horizon. Communists participated in democratic national elections and even sought to elect deputies to parliament. But such deputies were instructed to sabotage and disrupt the operations of the state from within. As an official Comintern declaration put it: "Communism repudiates parliamentarism . . . its aim is to destroy parliamentarism. Therefore it is only possible to speak of utilizing the bourgeois state organizations with the object of destroying them . . . The communist party enters such institutions not for the purpose of organization work, but in order to blow up the whole bourgeois machinery and the parliament itself from within" (*The Communist,* XI 2, pp. 186 ff.).

The communist attack was particularly severe against all progressive elements of the nation, the "reformists" who taught that social reform was a valid alternative to social revolution. Earl Browder denounced Roosevelt's New Deal as carrying out "more brutally than Hoover the capitalist attack against the living standards of the masses and the sharpest national chauvinism in foreign relations" (*The Communist,* XII 8, pp. 71 f.). In Germany communists concentrated their attacks upon the social democrats whom they called social fascists, and whom they characterized as a more serious enemy of the working class than the Nazis. Proposals for a "democratic front" against Hitler were dismissed with scorn as treason to the revolution (*International Press Correspondence,* May 26, 1933, pp. 497 f.). Indeed a spokesman of the Central Committee of the German communist party hailed Hitler's rise to power as really a victory in disguise, since it destroyed "all democratic illusions" and would free the masses "from the influence of the Social Democratic party," thereby accelerating Germany's march to the proletarian revolution (*Rundschau,* Basel, No. 10, 1933, pp. 201–226).

There was a change in communist policy when Hitler seemed intent on committing aggression against Russia. Then communists became the champions of the widest possible front of resistance to Hitler, and in foreign relations, of the doctrine of collective security. But the old line was reasserted following the Nazi-Soviet Pact; and once more communism became the active enemy of the liberal democratic state, at the very time when Hitler was in the process of waging war against it. The American communist party opposed aid to Britain, on the theory that there was no moral difference between the causes for which Nazi Germany and England were fighting. Indeed, communists called on Americans to "hope and strive for the mutual destruction of both combatants." Moreover, they opposed American rearmament, assuring America that she had nothing to fear from an aggressive Nazism since she was "surrounded by two oceans" (*The Communist,* XX 2, pp. 115–119). The same policy of revolutionary defeatism was pursued by the communists in England. The continuation of the war was denounced as contrary to the interests of the working people of the world, and they called for a negotiated peace with Hitler. For what interest could the proletariat have in a war which was not waged directly for the only valid social good, the proletarian revolution? *The*

Daily Worker, for instance, on February 1, 1940, analyzed the war thus: "Hitler repeated once more his claim that the war was thrust upon him by Britain. Against this historical fact there is no reply. Britain declared war, not Germany. Attempts were made to end the war, but the Soviet-German peace overture was rejected by Britain. All through these months the British and French governments have had the power to end the war; they have chosen to extend it" (cited by Arnold Nash, "Some Reflections on Marxist Communism," in *Christianity and Society,* Autumn, 1942, p. 32).

Marxist theory, moreover, played a disastrous role in world affairs by its anti-religious propaganda, no less than by its doctrines of class hatred. The anti-religious propaganda of communism was rooted in the fact that religion was not a value creation of the labor movement and was therefore necessarily hostile to it. This propaganda attacked one of the most deeply seated loyalties in man and evoked a fierce opposition which tended to discredit the cause of social reconstruction even when advocated in non-communist circles. The great ethical resources of religion which were available for the purpose of building a nobler world order came under insidious and unrelenting criticism, bringing paralysis to those who should have labored zealously for liberation and rebirth. Even mankind's inheritance of moral wisdom came under fire, on the ground that only the exigencies of the class struggle could create a genuine morality. As Lenin phrased it: "We deny all morality taken from superhuman or non-class conceptions. We say that this is a deception, a swindle, a befogging of the minds of the workers and peasants in the interests of the class-struggle of the proletariat. We deduce our morality from the facts and needs of the proletariat" (*Religion,* International Publishers, N.Y., 1933, pp. 47, 48). The talk of class liquidation was similarly tragic in that it induced fears not alone among the top but also among the middle layers of our society.

Because of these attacks on fundamental human loyalties, loyalty to the nation, loyalty to the ethical and religious tradition, and loyalty to the social stratum, communism became for vast numbers the symbol of mankind's great enemy, a symbol that Nazi-fascists were not slow in exploiting for their own ends. As Fredrick L. Schuman observes: "Experience demonstrates . . . that the quest for social justice and a more abundant life cannot attain its goal through the fostering of economic competition, social rivalry and political strife among classes, interests, and pressure groups. Where such efforts to build a new economy and a new society lead to social revolution, as in Russia, they may conceivably result in something resembling the announced objective, after a long interval of impoverishment and tyranny. Where the attempt falls short of such millennial catharsis, its only result is to arouse vain expectations among the underprivileged and to evoke a great fear among the pecuniary and aristocratic elite groups at the apex of the social pyramid. That fear, invariably shared by the chronically insecure middle class, is the matrix of fascism. From it have been born most of the evils of our time; reaction, despotism, intolerance, racial persecution and the whole tragic pattern of appeasement on the part of those interested only in saving civilization from communism. The fear is with us yet, even in the midst of a war in which we are saved from total defeat only by the heroic resistance of the Soviet Union. Its results in the future will be as ghastly as they have been in the past, if the sources of the fear are not removed by a wholly new approach to the problem of a just and viable social order" ("Total War For What," in *Threshold,* October, 1942, pp. 5 f.).

VI

In its distinctly religious form dualism appears in the dichotomy between the material and the spiritual, a doctrine which, as Reinhold Niebuhr has so often pointed out, is ultimately traceable to Greek ethics ("Marx, Barth and Israel's Prophets," in *Christian Century,* January 30, 1935). Here the world is regarded as evil by its very nature. Man, as a bodily creature, in so far as he is enmeshed in the world, partakes of that evil. The only salvation available to him is identification with the transcendent order of pure being, God. Most religious dualists acknowledge a relationship between God and the world. God, they generally assert, is redeeming the world but human decisions in history are not seen as decisive in the process of redemption. Man is the passive agent who must surrender himself to the will of God, Who will then lift him up to save him.

We have a glaring illustration of this dualism in the writings of Dr. D. R. Davies whose recent credo is stated in his new book *On To Orthodoxy*. This is but another strange port among many, including Christian liberalism, pacifism, Marxism, and humanism, where this restless spirit has sought refuge. A brief statement of his faith is given in an article in the *British Weekly* of September 21, 1939. Here he affirms: "I believe that man is radically evil, that sin is of the very texture of human nature. I believe that owing to that original inherent sin, man is incapable of creating a just society . . . ; that he is cursed by a fatal contradiction which ordains that the power by which he advances in civilization nullifies and destroys his progress."

A similar pessimism permeates the thinking of Karl Barth and, on another level, it is likewise present in the writings of Reinhold Niebuhr. It is true that Barth has recently spoken with prophetic decisiveness on man's duty in the current world tragedy. As for Professor Niebuhr, his grappling with the problems of social ethics has been one of the great triumphs of contemporary religion in America. Nevertheless the logic of a pessimistic interpretation of human nature is to regard social catastrophe as the product of what is irredeemable in man and, therefore, unavoidable.[1] Such religion, as Niebuhr himself once observed in criticizing the pessimism of the German religious tradition, will tend to express itself in "extra-ethical" terms ("Europe's Religious Pessimism," in the *Christian Century,* August 27, 1930).

It is essentially the same dualism which is responsible for the hypostasis of certain moral terms which, like Platonic ideas, are endowed with an existence apart from the tangled web of human affairs in the arena of history. Thus in August, 1941, a religious periodical called upon its readers to pray for peace, expounding: "Someone asks, 'Are you praying simply for a cessation of hostilities?' And an-

[1] Dr. Niebuhr's revised statement of his position, in *Human Destiny,* the second volume of his Gifford Lectures, appeared after Dr. Bokser's lecture was delivered.—The Editor.

other, 'Are you praying for a peace that means a Hitler victory?' And another, 'Are you praying for a peace through a British victory?' And still another, 'And are you praying to keep America out of war, even if America's entrance into war is the only way to destroy Hitler and his menace of world conquest?' . . . These are questions for the wise men of politics and diplomacy to argue about. Everyone has his own personal idea of what is the best kind of peace. We are content to leave the answer with God . . ." (*The Parish Monthly,* Our Lady Queen of Martyrs Roman Catholic Church, Forest Hills, N.Y., XII, 8, p. 8).

And is not this dualism involved also in the withdrawal of certain religious perfectionists into a realm that transcends our tragedy and from which they will not descend into the mire of our troubled arena of history? From that perspective they see that every society presently locked in struggle is enmeshed in some sin and that since the choice before them is not one between absolute good and absolute evil, they will make no choice at all. They occasionally speak from the heights, but when they speak it is with the imperatives of an absolutist morality. The Reverend W. Burnett Easton, for instance, is unwilling to have the churches pray for victory in the current struggle. As he puts it: "The chief reason for not praying for victory is that we simply do not know whether an Allied victory, from God's perspective, is a good thing" (see discussion in *Christianity and Crisis,* October 5, 1942). The editor of the *Christian Century,* Dr. Charles Clayton Morrison, calls Christians supporting the nation's war effort "militarist Christians." He does not actively oppose the war, but he regards it beyond moral decision, an "unnecessary necessity," injected by the flow of events into the time process and demanding the citizen's collaboration and sacrifice. But such sacrifices are devoid of religious or moral significance (see for instance his editorial "Unnecessary Sectarianism," in *Christian Century,* November 11, 1942, and the collection of his editorials written since America entered the war, *The Christian and the War,* Chicago, 1942). Others have expounded a doctrine of pure love that has simply eliminated the distinction in the moral qualities of human conduct. One is reminded of the rejoinder by the Archbishop of Canterbury: "I notice some people who are always repenting of their father's sins and forgiving Germany for injuries done to Czechs and Poles; and I am not impressed" (cited in *A Righteous Faith For a Just and Durable Peace,* N.Y., 1942, p. 49).

This transcendentalism has also exterted an influence within Jewry, particularly among certain exponents of Reform Judaism. Identifying Jewish life exclusively with the universals of Jewish religious affirmation, these men have sought to negate the particularities of historical Jewish existence, including even religious ceremonials. Religion was to be cultivated as an abstract idea; the specific forms into which the idea was concretized in history were deprecated as "particularistic." Above all, these men have opposed a renewal of Jewish group life in Palestine. For such a Jewish group, functioning as an autonomous historical entity, would be confronted with the dilemmas and compromises that face all concrete existence; and this would do injury to the purely spiritual and universal, the untarnished ideas of an abstract Jewish faith.

The most articulate champion of this doctrine in contemporary Judaism, is Rabbi Morris S. Lazaron. He admits that Jews always professed a devotion to "Zion rebuilt," but that "was a prayer, a longing, a hope, a dream." Those Jews in the past, moreover, believed that "it must come about . . . by the work of God, not through the hands of men." It is when the dream becomes a project on which human hands begin to labor that it is made "unspiritual" and a menace. "A dream state is a dream, but a real state means defense, diplomacy, alliances and international politics. Zion can be an informing exalting spiritual motivation in Jewish life in the future as it has been in the past, without politics." Rabbi Lazaron is not unmindful of the current Jewish world tragedy and of the contribution that Palestine might make toward alleviating it, but he remains undaunted in his universalism. "Others say," he acknowledges, " 'Save the Jewish people!' Yes! But I am not interested in saving the Jewish people as a people unless in their hearts there burn the fires of the old faith, the psalmist's longing for God, the prophets' social passion and the rabbinical challenge to life's disciplines" (*Common Ground,* N.Y., 1937, pp. 66, 114, 128). This is, of course, a departure from the authentic Jewish tradition, which is uncompromisingly monotheistic.

It is a Judaism reformed in the direction of the dualistic heresy, in which the abstract idea alone is regarded as good, while all concrete existence is negated as the source of evil.

It is of men such as these that Dr. Henry Sloane Coffin has written: "They will have the Kingdom of Heaven or nothing . . . We can only expect and work for some approximation of the divine ideal—the best we can contrive under the circumstances. But absolutists abhor these relative goods, with their admixture of evil. And when men refuse to work with the best they can get under given conditions they force something far worse on mankind" (*Christianity and Crisis,* November 16, 1942, p. 2).

A religion that divides reality into such a fatal dualism cannot function adequately as a force for an ethical reordering of life. For the transcendental order of pure being becomes another form of other-worldliness, a refuge from the sordid problems of history, and pragmatically, a diversion from immediate social responsibilities. The religion that will help establish and maintain a valid and viable world order will be a religion of uncompromising monotheism, that will not reject any part of being, of man or of the world, from the creative goodness of God. Such a religion will not seek a refuge from the world, but it will endow men with the vision and the energy to serve as partners of God in the work of creation which is forever being renewed when we help subdue chaos and anarchy and bring life under the sovereign rule of God's law of universal righteousness and love.

VII

A crisis is the ultimate test not alone of human hearts, but also of the faiths by which men live. Under the impact of the rod, the scales fall from human eyes and we tend to see with new clarity what is true and what is false. The current world tragedy has long been in the making. But behind each fatal deed has been the fatal idea. While a cancerous growth was forming in the body of our society, men were being misled by a false diagnosis. Some felt secure in their private reservation, asking only that we make firmer the fence that separates us from the rest of the world. Others sought a scapegoat; and they found it—the Jew. In smug contentment they heard the tales of the Nazis and their fellow-travelers. The more weird the tale, the more confident they felt. For the sins of the world would not go unrequited; there was someone who could be made to expiate them . . . And the Marxists, meanwhile, labored for the revolutionary cataclysm. The only element of sanity injected into their thinking was the stake they had acquired in history, the Soviet Union. But beneath the varieties of Marxism's fluctuating strategy, there continued the old tribalism, the old apotheosis of a fragment of the human community, the idealized proletariat. And those who were the custodians of the truth that could have brought healing became, as it were, transfixed by the dazzle, the shining luster of the truth, and spent themselves in ecstatically admiring it, instead of administering it. Meanwhile the cancer grew larger. And when the patient required surgery, some of the doctors were holding back because, forsooth, how can you cut the flesh of one whom we are bidden to love! The divine rod has accordingly smitten harder. More men are now marching toward the truth, but it is by the light of our civilization in flames.

Blueprints for a new world order are coming from many directions. With the technical details of the plans we cannot concern ourselves. But we shall fail once again unless we reckon with the truths of man's nature. As seen from the perspective of Judaism, man is an organ in the larger human organism, the universal community of mankind. He is, in the metaphor of Rabbi Judah Loew of Prague (1515–1609) a single piece of foliage upon the mighty tree which comprehends all life (Derek ha-Hayim, ch. 5). But the universal community functions in history through differentiated, particularized communities which are also organically related to it. The tension of individuals and groups is the means by which we enrich the total life of the human community with the unique resources of wisdom and life which inhere in the differentiated parts. But the health of the part is determined by and in turn determines the health of the whole. The tension of parts will continue; it is one of the creative sources in all human culture. But as we grow in wisdom we shall learn to integrate all the parts in a pattern of universal harmony so that the tensions will have their proper play but without the outbursts of violence and strife.

The structure of world organization that will achieve this integration will give political expression to the fact of the universal interdependence of all life; it will have to function on a world scale, inaugurating some form of world government. But it will not be a cosmopolitan world state dissolving the rich diversity of culture and of life prevailing among the varied peoples of the world. Indeed, its success will ultimately depend on the extent to which it will make available to diverse individuals and groups the requisite resources for the full flowering of their unique potentialities.

The root of world order lies, in other words, in world justice, a state of organization where each unit of human life enjoys the means with which to grow into the full maturity of its powers and uses those powers, in turn, as the means with which to serve the collective human community. In such an order there will be no room for submerged classes or individuals, for colonial or cultural or racial or class imperialisms. In such an order, there will be a place, after a great purging, for Germany and Japan, no less than for other men. In such an order there will be a new place for Israel, too. A democratic citizenship in each country will enable Jews, as other men, to function freely as members of a continuing cultural and religious fellowship; and for the Jewish people as a people there will also be made available that patch of soil where it may take root as a historic entity and grow freely toward the sun, for its own and the larger human blessing. The prophetic dream of a Jewish return to Palestine within the framework of a universal society of justice and love among all man will at last become a reality.

The establishment of the ideal of world organization does not involve the imposition upon men of goals and values which are inconsistent with human nature; it involves, on the contrary, a fuller reckoning with it; for by nature man's life is both universal and particular, and the two fuse into a harmonious unity. In the words of Rabbi Abraham Isaac Kook, the late chief rabbi of Palestine: "The more closely one studies the characters of individual human souls, the more baffled one becomes over the great differences between personalities . . . It is, however, precisely through their differentiations that they are all united toward one objective, to contribute toward the perfection of the world, each person according to his special talent. Surely one must marvel at the higher wisdom, through which by an inner mysterious power known only to God, these opposites are integrated and related one to the other, so that through the fusion of all the diverse minds and physiognomies there emerges a unified structure of consummate harmony" (Olat Rayah, Jerusalem, 1939, p. 388).

Nor are these goals and values inconsistent with the true interests of any human being. In the world reordering herein called for, individual men and nations will have to surrender certain power, economic or political, which they may have over other men. But the price by which that power may be maintained is continued social chaos and human strife, in which, on another level, those who wield that power are victimized as much as those who are held down by it; while the reward for its surrender is a world in which all men and all nations will have the opportunity of self-realization, of living out their lives to the full dignity of their promise, in peace and in fellowship with all other men.

Whether we shall finally reorder life in accordance with this vision will depend, among other things, on the rethinking of fundamentals that must go on in this stage of human transition. The cause of a new world order rests not on the wishful thinking of visionary sentimentalists, but on a cosmic imperative, or in the words of the religious tradition, on the will of God; and any world order built in defiance of this vision, no matter how technically imposing, will forever break down under the wrath of the divine judgment. Little men may laugh at our ideal. But the God of history is ever transmuting such laughter into tears and those tears into the song of a new redemption. If we fail, the rod will strike again and yet again. But Judiasm assures us that amid the pain and pathos of human striving, history is moving to a great realization. What lies ahead is not an endless recurrence of strife but the divine commonwealth of universal justice, freedom, and peace.

THE POLITICAL BASIS OF RECONSTRUCTION

By

ROBERT M. MacIVER, Ph.D.

Professor of Political Philosophy and Sociology,
Barnard College and Columbia University

One of the reasons why I was somewhat hesitant about accepting this topic is that I did not know what to include or what to leave out, where I should begin or where I could end. The political basis of reconstruction is pretty inclusive. You have already had three addresses on postwar reconstruction in this series. You are going to have several more. All of them have a political aspect, inevitably. So I was a little doubtful as to what I ought to take up particularly in the series. In my doubts and hesitations, I decided to cling strongly to the word "basis." So what I am going to try to do is to put before you what appear to me to be some fundamental considerations concerning the state, concerning what we must do and what we must think about the state itself if we want a better order of society, and for the first time an international order.

I claim that we have to rethink this thing we call the state and then, having rethought it, we have to remake the state in certain ways; for, in certain ways we have let the state get away from us. We have let the state get out of hand, get out of gear with our needs, with the needs of our civilization. When we think of the state we have traditions that need to be revised. We have beliefs that need to be challenged. We have institutions that have to be changed—some possibly abolished—and new institutions have to be created.

With that in mind, I want to put before you two fundamental

propositions regarding the political basis of reconstruction. The first proposition is that if we want a genuine international order we must change our notions about the thing we call sovereignty. Since the time of the Renaissance the countries of the western world have exalted "sovereignty." They have called it by various names. They have called it supreme, final, ultimate. They have said it was bound by no other powers of its own rank. They have said that it was subject to no obligations other than those it chose to acknowledge. They have regarded this thing called sovereignty as the final reach of law, the final realm of authority in the secular world.

In doing so they have often given it even mystical attributes. I want to say as emphatically as I can that there is no ground whatever for these attributions of sovereignty, except our willingness to believe them. It does not matter how many philosophers, how many jurists say this thing is so. That does not make it so, for a very simple reason—that the thing we exalt as the sovereignty of the state is a human institution, not a fact of nature. If it were a fact of nature we would try to learn about it scientifically, discover what it is, and then tell people. If it is a human institution, we do not do that. That is not the way we learn about it.

Sovereignty is nothing more than the authority that government possesses, the government of the state. It is nothing more than the power we allow government to possess, the power with which we invest the government. Sovereignty is not a thing that exists in nature and is not a thing that exists in its own right. Sovereignty, as a form of authority, has one peculiar property; to wit, there can be in any territory only one political authority regulating any particular department of human affairs. And in any territory, whatever political authorities exist within the whole territory must somehow be unified if you are going to have order and authority.

The authority of the state must have that peculiar property, that it is unified, and in that sense one within any territory. You can have as many creeds as you like in a country, in a territory, but you can only have one criminal code. You can have as many schools of thought, as many diversities of opinion, as many interest groups as you like in any one territory, but you can have only one civil code; you can have only one treaty-making power; you can have only one tariff-making power; and so on.

That is the peculiar thing about political authority, and that peculiar thing has been grossly distorted and magnified into the thing we call sovereignty. As you read the history of political thought, you find people saying (since the time of Bodin) that this thing called sovereignty is one and indivisible. And they add other attributes such as unlimited, omnicompetent, and all the rest of it. No American should cherish that delusion, because in this country sovereignty is not one and indivisible any more than it is unlimited or omnicompetent. Sovereignty is divided in this country, genuinely divided.

There are certain things that the component states can do that the Federal Government cannot do. There are certain things that the Federal Government can do that the component states cannot do. It is a divided sovereignty. If the governor of a state refuses, for example, to exercise his prerogative of pardon, there is no power under the Constitution, or, if you like, on this earth, that can compel him to do it. In various matters the individual state is supreme, but in other matters it is very far from being supreme. All you have to do is look at the number of statutes that are declared unconstitutional from year to year to see how unsupreme it is.

In this country, then, sovereignty is not one and it is not indivisible. To be sure, even in this country the writers of law books still repeat this ancient dogma. But sovereignty is not omnicompetent and it is not unlimited. It need not be, as the political system of this country shows.

If you go next and look at sovereignty from the outside, look at the state as against other states, again there is equally no reason why the thing called sovereignty should be unlimited, except that we like to think it is so, or are under the tradition of thinking it is so. If it is contrary to the needs of our civilization that the sovereignty of a state in relations with other states should be unlimited, there is nothing except our beliefs that prevents it from being unlimited, nothing in this world. If sovereignty is limited within the state, why on earth should it be unlimited when the issue is the relation of a state to other states?

Personal liberty does not mean that you or I are under no law, that you or I can do as we like. We do not think of that as personal liberty. No more should national liberty, the liberty of the state, mean that the state can do what it likes, that it also is under no law. That is the fetish of sovereignty we have to abandon. It is very important, I claim, as a basis for reconstruction that we abandon this notion.

We must be willing to give up—I will not say sovereignty, but the belief in it. We must be willing to enter with other states into one international order if we want to have a better kind of world politically than the one we have. We must be willing so to arrange things that the relations between states will themselves come under law, so that law will not end at the frontiers of the state. The relations between states must come under law just as the relations of persons come under the law, if we are going to have a decent world. We must abandon, in other words, the foolish notion that what any country does is its own affair, that it has something called a right to do what it likes. There is no right of that sort that ever can exist—there is no right without obligation.

If we need to make a constitutional change in this country to enable us to enter a world order in that sense, then we must demand that constitutional change. There is no way short of that. Otherwise, we will remain exposed, no matter what else we do, to a rule of force, a rule of war. If we want peace and liberty, the peace that goes with liberty, we must give up something that we have thought of without any particular reason as our sovereign rights, in so far as these are asserted in our relations with other states.

The time has more than come when we need seriously to face the question of building a greater law than the law of the state, a greater law that will include all states in their relations to one another. We ought not to shrink back to isolation when this war is over, as we did after the First World War. If we find that we cannot keep out of war, as we do find, then we must not be so foolish as to try to keep out of the peace making, the peace holding, the peace keeping that can help to prevent war.

But I want to turn from that first proposition to my second one. If we want a better world politically, then we must set the community clearly above the state. That is putting it very shortly and it may not mean much until I try to interpret it. We must, I say, clearly put the community above the state.

Of course, in one sense, that is the exact opposite of the totalitarian doctrine. The latter coordinates everything—churches, trade unions, organizations of every kind, every interest, every group, everybody, everything. When that happens, the state becomes the master of the community, swallows it up, and, then human personality and human dignity mean nothing any more so far as government is concerned. Why? Because the human personality is fed and nourished by creative association. The state can regulate the common external affairs of all men, but if *everything* is put into uniform, then the faith and the vision of human beings, the changing lights and glimpses that they attain, the inner autonomy that is the last source of all values or of the preservation of all values, are crushed.

All essential liberty in the modern world depends upon free association. These free associations arise spontaneously everywhere under modern civilization. If we are going to keep the state as the servant or the agent of the community, there must be hands off free associations everywhere. We will agree on some aspects of that very easily, but I want to press it a little further. We all agree that the state must not interfere with or control the religion of the people. We say, "Oh, yes, fine." Are we willing to carry that same principle all the way?

Let me add, the state must not control the morals of the people. Do you equally agree with me now? I maintain it is exactly the same principle.

Of course, I am not talking about the prohibition of acts that do definite injury or harm to our fellow men, to their persons, to their property, and so forth. These acts we must prohibit not merely because they are in our view immoral, but because they specifically violate the integrity, violate the equal rights of other men. It is quite a different ground of action.

Apart from that area which comes properly under the criminal code, the morals of groups vary as the religions of groups vary. Every group has its own morality, and we have no right to force our morality on other groups, any more than we have a right to force our religion on them. We have no right to make them good our way, if it is not their way, and there is no question of specific hurt against a fellow man.

A religious faith should be chary of calling in the police arm to support its moral values if they are not those of the community, or if they are those of a group only. It should be exceedingly chary, and sometimes we offend grievously in that way.

There is a broader side to all this. In any modern civilization we have to admit as equally necessary, two kinds of loyalty, two kinds of unity. There is one loyalty, one unity, that is shared by all men who live in the same territory, up from the village to the nation. There is another loyalty, another unity, that is shared by all who accept the same creed, who are moved by the same doctrines, who belong to the same school of thought, who accept the same creative principle, whatever it is.

Every man needs both, and it is the essence of human liberty, in the kind of society we now possess, that we do not force these two unities, these two loyalties, into one bracket, that we do not make the one the condition of the other. The state claims our loyalty. So does the cultural value, the belief, the religion, the creed, the cause, the mission we accept. A truly democratic state will respect these differences of value, because they are an inner bond of unity; apart from anything else, they are a bond of unity and a source of strength to men.

The only way to defeat the forces of reaction, I claim, the forces that hate difference, that want a simple unity, it to make the state the servant of the community and to distinguish carefully at all points these two kinds of loyalty, these two bases of union among men.

In that connection, we should remember that we live in a house of many mansions, or, if you like, we belong to a multi-group society. And some people do not like that, either because they have petty little minds, or because they have masterful minds. They want more unity. They want a more unified society. They think that multiplicity spells disorganization. They think that way, because they can think of unity only in terms of a primitive tribe. Multiplicity is not disorganization. It is the first condition of effective or durable organization in a modern society.

If that is so, then it means that all groups, in terms of their different values, or different creeds, must have equal rights of existence, not only politically, or legally, but socially and economically and spiritually, so far as the state is concerned and so far as our relations man to man are concerned.

Discrimination in this respect, the brand of inferiority which we attach to race, or religion, or nationality, or color, or any other difference, is the primary menace to a free society in the world we live in today. Because we have a multi-group society we must have democracy. To seek for any other form of unity is to follow the swastika. If we say we follow democracy, then we must, if we are going to be true to it, abandon discrimination everywhere.

I see my time is nearing its close. I put before you two rather broad propositions regarding the political basis on which we must, I maintain, reconstruct our somewhat shattered world. In doing so, I left out, of course, a great many important considerations. I have not referred, for example, to a single economic aspect. All these things come up elsewhere in your course. I have tried to deal with one or two things that seem to me to constitute the elements of the framework of an ordered society. It is within that framework, I claim, that we must apply our practical proposals of every kind.

Before I leave this subject, however, I would like to say that there is one preliminary before we can seek to build this more ordered and better society. World order is what we need. World order means world organization. World organization means the willing cooperation of the nations, certainly of all the greater nations of the world. You cannot get that kind of cooperation unless you have a certain kind of peace settlement when the time comes. If you have a peace settlement that goes in for territory, spoliation, revenge, retribution, or domination, no matter under what fine names, then you cannot have a world organization.

We have to choose one of two things: There are certain inevitable passions and feelings that belong to the time of war. There are other feelings that must dominate the peace if it is going to be a different kind of thing. We must be willing, when the time comes, to sacrifice the one to the other, or we will not have any willing cooperation of the states of the world, and we will have something abortive and perhaps worse than nothing, as we had after 1918.

Here, it seems to me, there is a peculiarly important task falling upon all churches and all religions. They must stand for generosity, for good will, when the time comes. They must stand for the conditions that make for good will among men, not thinking of the moment but thinking of the longer span of time. They must resist the spirit of revenge and retribution and spoliation. If they do, then they will render their own special and most necessary service to the building of a better world, and they cannot prepare too soon to start on that vital mission.

THE ECONOMIC BASIS OF RECONSTRUCTION

By

RAYMOND LESLIE BUELL, Ph.D.

Round Table Editor of "Fortune"

At the end of this war the potentiality will exist of great economic expansion, both at home and in foreign countries. War is a great destroyer not only of men but of capital. War also brings about, unconsciously perhaps, but nonetheless actually, great technological change and progress. This country and the other countries will need an entirely new technological foundation when this war is over, which ought to mean an improved standard of living for us all.

When I say there will be a great potential demand for expansion, involving investment and employment, I do not mean to imply that that demand will be automatically realized. The great problem before us is how to convert this potential demand into an effective demand that depends very largely on public policy, because economic activity is no longer automatic in the old sense. It can be repressed or it can be stimulated by the kind of policy and the kind of government we have, not only in this but in other countries.

To determine what kind of a public policy we ought to have we must do two things. First, we should define our economic goals, and second, we should define the methods by which we hope to realize such goals. Now the goals of the postwar period are quite obvious. We want in the first place full employment, or at least a reasonable approach to full employment. I do not believe that the people of this country will ever tolerate the condition which existed during the 'thirties in which ten million men or more were chronically out of work. I think that condition must be excluded from the range of political possibilities. We must accept a government responsibility, if it cannot be discharged by other agencies, for what I call reasonably full employment.

The second thing that we wish is improved living standards. We have had tremendous progress during the past century in the production of things which people consume, in improving the material basis of life which must be the basis of culture. But want is not yet abolished.

The third thing that we want is freedom; freedom of the individual, and freedom of minorities, not in the old negative sense, perhaps, but in the sense of an opportunity for self-expression even though that differs from the prevalent mood.

It is going to be very difficult to realize these three objectives; and in my opinion it depends very much on the kind of public policy we envisage at the end of this war. We will be confronted first with what is called the transition problem, and secondly, with the more ultimate problem of developing enough outlets for investment, public and private, to create fairly continuous opportunities for jobs.

Most economists today agree that employment depends upon investment, not so much upon the consumption of goods as upon the investment of money in new enterprises, which in turn create consumer goods.

In some ways the problem of the transition is going to be much more difficult to solve than the ultimate problem. The problem of transition comes down to this: In this country we are going to have between twenty-five million and forty million people in war activity, either in the armed services or in war plants, who will have to be reabsorbed in peacetime employment. We will have to reconvert our economy from a wartime basis to a peacetime basis. If that task is done poorly then the danger of a Fascist dictatorship in this country will become very real, under whatever name it is called. But if the job is done well, then I think we will have developed concepts and policies which will make the long-term solution infinitely easier.

As I see it, there are two dangers confronting this country in the solution of this transitional problem. The first danger will come, as it is already coming, from the extreme right. You read no doubt last week the speeches at the National Association of Manufacturers which reflected eagerness to get rid of all government controls the minute fighting stops—with the exception of the speech by Mr. Prince of General Electric.[1] No doubt that will be the temper of the country.

The controls which we must accept in wartime, represented by rationing and the limitation upon automobiles and tires, under any circumstances are irksome, but when the rationing seems to be done poorly and administration seems to be bad, popular discontent increases. It is going to be very easy at the end of this war to say we must get rid of all controls immediately. Many conservatives will say that unless we do that the New Deal, the bureaucracy in Washington, is going to clamp down these controls as a permanent way of life and thus end the American system.

What would happen if we followed the road of the extreme conservatives? Well, I think this would happen. We would have in the first place an enormous inflation, because we are now accumulating excess purchasing power in the form of war bonds and bank deposits, which are now held in check but which will be dumped on the consumer market as soon as the war is over. If there are no controls in the postwar period you will find a bidding up of consumer goods such as automobiles, which will drive prices upward and get us inflation, which we are now trying to avoid. It is popular to say that we had a large inflation in World War I, but in fact, the big inflation came in the year after the war, the year when we took the controls off, and it was that inflation which did so much to unsettle conditions in the 'twenties.

There is going to be a serious conflict in the immediate postwar period between the desire of people in this country to get back to the consumer market and buy an automobile, and the international need of sending materials to the devastated countries of Europe to help them get on their feet. It is going to take the wisest leadership in the country to resolve that conflict without disaster to our-

[1] The reference is to the meeting held in December, 1942.

selves as well to the peoples abroad. I am not at all optimistic that we will solve that in a statesmanlike way.

The second danger from the right is that under our existing political system we will see a new demand for high tariffs and government subsidies. Probably at no time in our period have the forces driving us toward self-sufficiency been so strong as today. The very necessities of war are creating high-cost industries and high-cost branches of agriculture, such as domestic fats and oils, synthetic rubber and sugar beets. We are building high-cost plants all over the country as a war necessity. Unless our political system becomes purified, I am quite sure that after the war the congressmen from each district will be waited on by representatives both of management and labor in these plants, who will say to them, "We have a good thing in our district. This war plant has been paying good wages. It is making good profits. It is good for the district. We know that the war is over but we hope you can get us some subsidy or tariff or something like that to keep us going." I think in the absence of a distinct change in our American politics we are likely to get that. Well, if we get those two things, an unrestricted inflation, and a new outburst of high tariffism, I think we will have a boom, but it is bound to be followed by an even greater collapse than in 1929. The government will have to step in either to prevent that collapse or to offset it later. As a consequence I think we would go to the left much farther than if the extreme right does not have a decisive voice when the war ends.

If that is a danger from the extreme right there is an equal danger from the left. That danger, I think, comes from a group of people who believe that America needs a permanent War Production Board in Washington to allocate the productive resources of this country by government fiat instead of by the competitive market. There is no doubt one wing of the Administration in Washington today which would like to have that concept of a rigidly controlled economy made permanent. Those people would like to see the peacetime economy of this country supported by indefinite deficit financing. They do not admit it, but as far as I am concerned, the only outcome of that method will be some form of socialist dictatorship.

Well, what is wrong with a socialist dictatorship? The very fact that the intellectual movement for socialism has collapsed throughout the world, I think is an admission that something is quite wrong with it. My views can be stated quite simply: Socialism simply means bureaucracy, as we have seen it today in the war, multiplied a thousand times. That kind of bureaucracy cannot produce goods nearly as efficiently or as cheaply, or in the variety consumers wish, as can a market economy. The second thing I think most people find incompatible with socialism is the concept of freedom. I do not think that a socialized economy can be a democratic economy. The very extension of our present bureaucracy under the guise of the war effort, the OPA and the rent control and things like that, creates very numerous and very serious political problems throughout the country. If you get, as we have been tending to get in the past ten years, a large percentage of population on the government payroll or dependent upon handouts for their economic welfare, it is very difficult to get the degree of political independence and individualism that we need if we are really to develop the concept of democracy and the idea of equality of opportunity.

Well, it is evident from what I have said that I would like to see this postwar economic problem solved through private initiative. But that does not mean that I think it is possible or desirable to return to the *laissez faire* economics and politics of the nineteenth century. Private initiative can operate only under modern conditions subject to three provisos. One is that it accept rather heavy social obligations, which will have to be imposed upon it by the state. The second is that it will be willing to accept a kind of competition from which it has tended to shy away. And I would add a third proviso: that industry must be willing to accept the principle of collective bargaining with organized labor to a far greater extent than before. These are the three conditions which seem to me implicit in any effort to restore private enterprise at the end of this war: rather heavy social obligations, a new concept of competition and low prices, and an acceptance of the principle of collective bargaining which some industrialists in this country still in their hearts oppose. Subject to these conditions, I believe that it is possible to get the postwar expansion that all of us want, this improved standard of living and full employment, very largely through the resumption of the activities of the private industrialists as well as the demands of the consumer on the market.

But to do that I think that we in this country must revise very radically our policies along three lines. In the first place there can be no long-run private recovery at the end of this war unless we change our tax system. I do not mean that we must necessarily lower taxes, although presumably that will be done. Nevertheless the tax policy of the past ten years has tended to repress risk taking, and venturesomeness, and has penalized men who have gone out and erected factories and created new jobs in contrast to men who put their money in tax-exempt bonds or industrial bonds, and sit at home and do nothing except play golf. That tax system must be changed if we expect to see real private expansion. That does not necessarily mean that we must lower the taxes on very wealthy men, but it does mean that a wealthy man who is willing to take his money and risk it on a new invention or idea, creating new jobs, ought to have to pay much less tax than a man who does nothing but sit around at his club and clip coupons.

The second change we must have is in our labor policy. I have said that labor unions must be accepted, but labor unions have got the same responsibilities to the public as industry and some labor leaders today are in the same type of irresponsible position as were the robber barons in this country fifty years ago. That statement may be too extreme, but I do think that unions in their formative period, when they are fighting for their existence, are bound to develop certain qualities of leadership which they will discard once their position is assured. There are obvious things in the labor movement in this country which are a scandal. I refer to labor racketeering on the one hand and communism on the other. I see no justification whatever for those things, and if labor unions themselves do not eliminate them legislation and the police will do it for them.

But I come now to a more difficult problem and that is what I call the general restrictive attitude of certain labor unions in this country. By that I mean the attitude that it is to their interests to hold down production, a monopolistic attitude identical with that of the industrial leader, the idea that a man should lay only so many bricks a day, or that a spray should not be used in painting a house, or that featherbed rules on the railroads are a good thing. All such devices to make work and increase costs are elements which increase prices to the public and tend to bring about unemployment just as much as do industrial monopolies. And the stronger labor becomes in this country, the greater its power becomes of doing damage unless it changes this psychology.

What I have said is not true of all unions. Certainly among the craft unions there is a greater tendency to restriction than there is among the industrial unions, but the attitude is so widespread as to justify speaking about it rather openly.

The same thing is true, I think, of wage rates. Hitherto the most obvious justification of a labor union has been to push up wage rates. Well, all of us want higher wages, but if a wage increase merely leads to a price increase, you again get into a situation where the volume of goods which the public will buy declines, instead of working for maximum consumption. A wage rate pushed beyond a certain point again leads to reduction and with that you begin to get unemployment.

I would like to see new mechanisms set up in the country whereby labor unions as well as employers could look to their enlightened interests and really talk about these questions from the standpoint of the public as well as from that of their own immediate needs. If we could get a national organization of employers, as we already have a national organization of the workers, and then get them around the table to talk about these things, we might get progress. But the danger of that is that you simply get a national monopoly on both sides which would exploit the public. That is what is already beginning to happen in England, and for that reason I think you must have some form of government leadership. I would like to see a national economic advisory council in which all these groups would get together around a table under a public chairman and try to see how closely they can agree upon a common economic policy. I think that would do much to stop the ceaseless and ruinous competition of economic lobbies in Washington today. But at any rate I do say that we will need a different attitude on the part of a number of labor leaders and unions in the country, as well as of a number of employers, if we are going to realize our goal of full employment.

In my opinion those two concrete things are of the greatest importance as far as getting domestic revival in the country after this war is concerned: a new tax concept and a new labor concept.

I am willing to admit that if private industry does not provide full employment, government has got to take care of the unemployed. I have already stated that we must have a system of social security. But I want to make this observation: that whenever any society puts social security above opportunity and expansion, it begins to enter into a period of decay. For the first time in our history America during the past ten years elevated security to a position above opportunity and responsibility, and I am very much afraid of the same tendency in British life today. All of us admire the purpose of the Beveridge Report, but the astonishing thing to me was that Mr. Beveridge said only last week, "I have no idea how England is going to solve the unemployment problem after this war." [2] My point is that unless we do get a concept of production, of how to keep men at work in producing goods, no social security system can be of any great value.

And I would say that a further difficulty is that the kind of taxation system many people propose to finance social security is of such a nature that it tends to repress the private production of wealth, and the risk taking which I mentioned.

Some of you no doubt have read Arnold Toynbee's great study of history. Well, his whole thesis in his analysis of the rise and fall of the twenty-one civilizations of the world, is that a new civilization or a great civilization is a product not of ease, a product of orthodox uniformity, but rather of adversity, of an intense struggle

[2] This lecture was given on December 15, 1942.

against one's environment or against geographic or physical or inhuman conditions which it takes a tremendous effort to overcome. And he adds a very interesting section on what he calls the "Stimulus of Wars," in which he shows that a very great war induces a country to put forth gigantic effort to win the war and in the process it releases energies which usher in a new flowering of its life. And the great example of that was the victory of Athens over the Persians in the Battle of Salamis. At the end of that victory Athens and Greece entered upon that great epoch which today is known as Greek Civilization.

We may be in such a period today. Mr. Toynbee would not justify war as a stimulus to civilization. Nevertheless we have been going through a period of ten years of stagnation in this country in which we have talked about security and guaranteeing everybody against the adversities of life, and even including death if you will read the reports of the National Resources Planning Board. It may be that this gigantic war effort we now have to put forth is going to wake us up, be a stimulus which will overcome many of these static conceptions, and usher in an era of economic expansion which obviously goes along with cultural realization and development. But to do that we have got to have a different concept of the world than we have had in the past.

I have talked so far about the domestic situation, but it is necessary also to have a new concept of international society. That means, roughly, that the idea of shielding ourselves against foreign competition has got to be modified. If this country wants any kind of world economic expansion, we must be willing to allow imports to enter the country if we want to have exports. Now it is to our interest to want exports. At the end of this war the whole world is going to be crying for mass-production goods which America can make. We can have an enormous market, we can bring about a world economic expansion such as England did in the nineteenth century, but only on one condition: that we are willing to take goods and services in return. We have not been willing to do that and as a result we have unconsciously given away about forty billion dollars worth of goods since 1914. When we wake up and discover what we have done we get very angry about it and become very anti-foreign. I do not believe the American people will consciously give away what they give unconsciously. But the fact is that we cannot return to the economic policy of the 'twenties and 'thirties. There must be a willingness to reduce tariffs and to import if we want to export.

This brings up a question of great political importance, and I will touch on it only hurriedly. Take the situation in England. Despite the Beveridge Report, the economic position of England at the end of the war is going to be very difficult. This war is wiping out her foreign investments. It is destroying her merchant marine. Hitherto Britain has paid for her imports in large part by interest on her investments and by her shipping. She will not be able to do that after this war. In fact, to maintain her prewar standard of living, Britain will have to increase her exports by 75 per cent. That is going to be a gigantic task. Britain has two alternatives. She can join with us in parallel anti-depression policies, reduction of trade barriers, working for a free expansion of the world's economy on a so-called multilateral basis, or she can go out and fight for markets and create new agreements and engage in exclusive bargaining. For England this is a matter of life or death.

If we are willing to reduce our tariffs so that British goods can come into this market, if we are willing to embark upon an enlightened economic policy for the world, Britain will go along with us. But if we go into high tariffism, Britain will be forced by necessity to go out and struggle for markets and say, for example, to Argentina, "I will buy your beef, but you must in turn buy all your goods from me and not from the United States." The result would be that England and America would inevitably move apart both economically and politically. Sooner or later we would find ourselves in heated economic and diplomatic rivalry for the control of the postwar world. If that happened it would be a great catastrophe. I see no possibility of world reconstruction, economic or political, unless America and Britain come to terms. There is a very grave danger that we will split, not on India and a lot of things that our liberal friends talk about, so much as on this hard economic question, and that issue is coming up sooner than you think. It is going to arise in June in Congress, when the Hull Trade Agreements Act expires. The Administration will ask for a renewal of that Act, as a symbol of economic reconstruction, and the willingness of this country to play a part economically in the postwar world. The Republicans in Congress have always opposed that Act. This time they are going to be strong enough to kill it. I do not say they will kill it. There is a liberal wing of the Republican Party which is becoming stronger. I do say if they kill it the result is going to be catastrophic, not only in an economic sense, but in the wider political sense which I have mentioned.[3]

That roughly is my picture of the economic order I hope will arise out of this war. I want to see a world in which private initiative and energy are released for constructive purposes. That cannot be done without governmental leadership and constructive policies. I do not believe in any negative theory of the state. In this age in which we have so many organized groups warring against each other, so many gigantic skeins of thread to be unwound, the government is the one agency which in the last resort must have an overall responsibility. But that responsibility must be exercised (and here we must reverse the trends of the past ten years), not toward repressing energies, not toward stifling new ideas of risk taking, not toward favoring the immediate interests of this group against the other group; but rather toward a releasing process in which the immediate interests of groups are reconciled on behalf of the higher good. That may sound a little vague and idealistic. Nevertheless, since World War I we have had here what I would call abuses by the right for twelve years, followed by abuses by the left for the past twelve years. Now it looks as if we are moving back to the right, but if we are going to have another twelve years of abuses by the right—a continued oscillation of extremes—I see very little hope for us or for the world. I think we have got to find a synthesis of the good from the right and the good from the left, and try to

[3] Congress renewed the Act before the date of expiration.

build up a middle-ground position. If we do that, as I think we can, then I see real hope, not only for reconstruction in the old sense but for the ushering in of a period of civilization such as we have never had before.

THE CULTURAL BASIS OF RECONSTRUCTION

By

LAWRENCE K. FRANK, Esq.

In the very short time allotted here this morning, you realize it is rather difficult to do more than perhaps outline the problem and indicate some of the larger dimensions of the task which is indicated by the title, "The Cultural Basis of Reconstruction."

Since there is a general disposition to use the word "cultural" with a capital "C" to indicate art, music, literature, what a selected group of individuals possess as a refinement of life, I think it may be desirable to try to clarify the basic conception of culture, in terms not of what it is but of what it does. For that, it may be useful to seek a little deeper and longer time perspective. So I should like at the outset to invite you to consider the following.

If we stop and reflect, we will recognize that all over the earth there are groups of men, all belonging to the same species, *homo sapiens,* differing slightly in size, color, and some functional capacities, but fundamentally alike. We will also realize upon very brief reflection that despite the local peculiarities of climate, weather, flora and fauna and topography, fundamentally the earth is similar, uniform, regular, and consistent. Yet, against that background of similarity of man and of essential homogeneity and uniformity of what we call nature, we may contrast the picture of groups of men living in essentially different cultural worlds, worlds which are so different that they are usually incomprehensible to members of any other cultural group.

If we were to ask ourselves how it comes about that essentially the same kind of human beings, existing in a homogeneous world, yet live in such different cultural worlds, frankly, the answer, I should say, is that we do not know. There are no historical records of the very earliest days, and all that we can do is to offer some surmises and draw some inferences, especially inferences, from some of the so-called primitive cultures which are still available for scrutiny.

Just as we have had to speculate about the beginnings of living cells and organisms, so I believe we have to speculate about the beginnings of culture. May I, then, quite frankly offer this speculation, as one way of approaching the problem of getting a perspective?

I believe we can say that from the very earliest days man everywhere has faced certain persistent life tasks. Obviously, he had to come to terms with the environment if he were to survive, to derive food, shelter, protection for himself and for his offspring. Also, if he were going to live in any kind of group, he had to organize and maintain some scheme of group living as a society, in which there would be some order, some division of labor and some differentiation of functions, such as those between the male and the female.

Thirdly, he had to devise some way of regulating human behavior and physiological processes by transforming functional activities and impulsive behavior into orderly, patterned conduct that was compatible with the kind of group living or social order which he sought to maintain.

I venture to say that those are the three basic persistent life tasks that have faced man from the beginning, that face every generation anew. They create social problems that cannot be solved but only restated by every generation in terms of its knowledge, its insights, and particularly its sensibilities or sympathetic feelings.

In order to face those tasks, early man had to make certain assumptions. First, he had to make certain assumptions about the kind of world or the nature of the universe in which he found himself, how it operated, what made things happen, who controlled and directed it, and what was the power behind events; was it a malevolent universe or a beneficent universe?

Secondly, he had to make certain assumptions about his own place in that universe, in that world—where he came from, how he was created, what his relationship was to whatever power was assumed to control the universe, and whether he was within or without nature.

Thirdly, he had to make some assumptions about the relationship of the individual to this group life which he was endeavoring to establish, to answer the exigent question that faces us in all human relations; namely, who shall be sacrificed for whom? And along with that assumption about man's relationship to his group are a host of subsidiary assumptions or beliefs which we recognize in what we call the rights, titles, obligations and interests of our legal system.

And fourthly, he had to make certain assumptions about human nature and the image of himself, of what man himself was, whether good or evil, whether he was fixed or plastic, what kind of a person he was or might be.

I am suggesting for your consideration that in facing these three basic life tasks and in making these four fundamental assumptions, we have what might be called the dimensions of a culture, because each culture may be looked upon as a different approach to those three life tasks, a different formulation of these basic assumptions. These four basic assumptions reinforce each other, are interdependent and give sanction and credibility to each other. We find them in our culture, in the higher literate cultures, formulated in verbal terms usually, but they are found in all cultures, in whatever they have in the way of a religion, and they are expressed in their arts, in their philosophy, in so far as it may be articulately formulated, and in their legal procedures and their formulated laws. In addition, they are perpetuated and carried on in the use and wont of tradition, of the mores, what people believe, what they accept, what they themselves look to as the dimensions of their values and in the sanctions for all their practices and conduct.

What seems to be worth emphasizing here is this: that everywhere man, faced with the same nature, rejected a purely biological existence, living on the basis of merely functional activity and physiological impulse, and sought to create a human way of life, what we call a culture. That is the major point I would like to emphasize. Man everywhere has sought to create a human way of life, rejecting a mere organismic, mammalian, functional existence.

Food, fighting, procreation, were not enough for man with a large brain. While we may say that man was faced with necessity, with danger which spurred him on, I believe he was also faced with boredom, and he created his arts and created a large part of his culture because he could not tolerate a kind of existence consisting of merely eating, fighting, procreating and sleeping.

The significance of that viewpoint—if you are willing to bear with me as I develop it a little further—is that man everywhere has imposed upon nature the meanings, the significances, the values which he himself puts into nature. Nowhere do we find a bare geographical situation. It always has some peculiar meaning or significance. It is expressive of some of these basic assumptions and beliefs by which he has tried to give his life more meaning and significance than nature unadorned presents. And, in addition, we find that everywhere man has imposed upon himself patterns of conduct and feeling that involve coercion, compulsions, repressions, and aspirations.

In other words, this cultural viewpoint suggests that everything that happens, every event, every relationship, everything that man takes notice of, is ordered to these basic cultural dimensions, just as in our scientific enterprise the observations of natural phenomena are ordered to the mathematical fields, or conceptual frames of reference, which give them a significance and meaning. I should like to stress that analogy, because I think it is probably a good, dynamic picture of how man approaches nature and fits it into the patterns of his own belief, his own value judgments, and his own aspirations, and he also fits his own physiological activities and behavior into the patterns he has created for his own guidance. All of his impulses, all of his needs, eliminations, emotional impulse, sexual activities, have been patterned, regulated, repressed, elaborated, in ways that are astonishing when one comes to look at their amazing variations and adornments.

In other words, we can say that each culture has selected out of the totality of events and of the environment those aspects, those events, those dimensions which it has chosen to give meaning to, to give emphasis to, and those which it has chosen to ignore, just as it has put into the environment and living all the preferences and all the esthetic significance which each group has found therein.

Man has everywhere viewed events in terms of these four basic assumptions as to what kind of universe it is, how it is operated, and so on. Also we may say that each cultural group has developed what I have ventured to call a series of time perspectives, meaning by this that they have always seen the immediate present in terms of a retrospective time perspective of what has happened or is supposed to have happened before, and also in terms of a prospective time perspective of what is going to happen or is expected tomorrow and beyond tomorrow. So that each immediate present event derives its significance from what has gone before, and what is anticipated or sought in the future.[1]

This time perspective may be of greater or lesser depth, and we begin to get some of the basic differences between cultures when we think of their contrasting time perspectives. The Hindu time perspective is expressed in a notion of reincarnation, of an endless existence in which one perpetually seeks to achieve a higher existence, contrasted, let us say, with the Western European time perspective, the conception of a very short terrestrial life to be followed by an eternity either blissful or otherwise; but in respect to which man has only one chance.

Again, we may say that each culture has selected from all of man's many potentialities those which it has preferred to emphasize, to elaborate, to refine, to develop, and those which it has chosen to repress or ignore. When we examine other cultures we become suddenly aware of the extraordinary possibilities and potentialities of the human race which in our culture have largely been ignored or forgotten or treated as not having sufficient value or significance to be cultivated.

Each culture, may I say, has also created its own sensibility, its

[1] Cf. the writer's paper "Time Perspectives", *Journal of Social Philosophy,* 4:4 293–312. July, 1939.

own pattern of feeling as to how it will allow its sympathies to flow and recoil, what and whom it will cherish, to what and whom it will give value and significance, and what it will reject or deny. We see this in the attitude and behavior toward animals and persons and the differentiated attitudes toward individuals.

As I said before, these fundamental patterns are expressed most clearly in the arts, for the arts have been the vehicle, the medium, through which, to a larger extent than we perhaps realize, our basic religious, philosophical and ethical aspirations have been made really meaningful to us. These have been presented through painting, through poetry, through novels, through plays, through the plastic and graphic arts, which have directed our awareness and our feelings, have created our sensibilities. Moreover, the artists have created and made meaningful the symbols by which we live.

If you follow this view you may be prepared to accept the statement that culture is not a mysterious emanation or something existing somewhere between the earth and the sky; it is not a mechanism and it is not a superhuman organization. Culture is the complex patterns of belief, action, speech and feelings which have been historically developed and which primarily exist in man, in us. It is built into us in our childhood by what we are told to believe, to see, to think, to feel, to do, or not to do. It is built into us so that it becomes a part of us. As Margaret Mead has suggested, we are like fish unaware that we live in water, because our culture creates our whole environment, and it is almost impossible for us, without a tremendous effort, to become aware that we are living in a cultural world, that we ourselves create and maintain a cultural world by this continual imposition of value and significance and form upon an otherwise plastic world and plastic human nature.

Then, also, I think we should put into this picture the further aspect of cultures, that they provide for man a series of institutional practices and rituals, whereby he can conduct most of his activities, particularly his person-to-person relationships. So we have in our culture the practice of contract, barter, sale, employment, courtship, marriage, divorce, litigation, and a variety of highly patterned practices with appropriate symbols, like money, through which we conduct these relationships, which further help to give order and regularity to our group living.

If all human behavior is directed and controlled by these cultural formulations, and by these patterns of conduct, you begin to see how the diversity of human conduct, even the crimes and the mental disorders, are but variations upon the basic patterns. They are even realized and accepted by those who deny them, because they polarize themselves against the ideals of their own culture. Each culture by what it permits and what it forbids, what it encourages, what it represses, and especially by the way it treats its children and transmits these lessons to them, fosters a certain kind of personality-character structure, because personality is the individual's way of carrying that culture, his way of feeling about life, especially toward other individuals and toward himself. Personality is a process and may be defined, culturally, as the idiomatic way in which each individual organizes his experience and reacts with feelings to life, in accordance with the cultural patterns and teachings which have been given to him in his childhood and youth.

That is why we can say that culture is in us, and whatever we find in life of value, significance, whatever we find of beauty and grace, is there because our cultural traditions have helped us to find them and put them there.

We transform our otherwise bare and shabby organic existence into a human way of life by this continual daily re-creation of the ideals and aspirations, this utilization of the patterns of conduct which our traditions have told us is the way to conduct our life and make it something beyond organic existence.

And, conversely, we must recognize that if we have cruelty and destruction and exploitation, it is not something outside of our culture. It is another aspect, another expression of what our culture has done to human personality. I believe it is important to recognize this, because every culture, including our own, likes to emphasize its virtues, to proclaim its lofty aspirations, and parade its ethical formulations, and to ignore the wastage, the degradation, the humiliation, the warped, twisted, malevolent personalities whom it also fosters and who are also products of that culture.

We have a long tradition in Western European culture of individual responsibility and moral autonomy. That has been one of our great achievements. However, we are beginning to recognize that for individual responsibility and moral autonomy, we must provide the cultural formulations and the educational processes in childhood that will foster the personalities who can carry the burdens of freedom, who can maintain a society that fosters individual responsibility. We are getting some new insights which help us to realize that the people who are anti-social and destructive are usually the individuals who have been maltreated or neglected, and therefore have been denied the opportunity to be self-directing, responsible human beings of the kind necessary to social order. This viewpoint suggests that social order is not a superhuman mechanism or organization operating through large-scale social forces. Social order is that which we must achieve in our personal lives, in our group lives, by patterning our conduct and feelings in accordance with the dimensions and values and the sensibilities which we cherish as our ideals.

I have taken quite a time to give you what I think is essential to a discussion of the topic, "The Cultural Basis of Reconstruction," because we must begin to think in these cultural terms: that we are culture bearers, that we have a body of traditional assumptions and beliefs that have come down to us from the past, that we are trying to create social order and to regulate our personal lives and our group lives according to those traditional cultural formulations. We should try to remember this when we ask what is going to happen in the postwar European world; every one of the plans and programs for political and juridical reconstruction and the elaborate blueprints for economic regulation and control of financial reform, and so on, will have to be translated into action by people who are the products of the Western European culture, who bear within them these traditional patterns and whose personalities suffer from many of the distortions, the warped, twisted feelings, the frustrations and self defeats, which are so frequent in Western European culture.

After going over many postwar reconstruction programs, I am

struck by the way we set up these paper programs and blueprints. I begin to wonder whether we are not all impelled to do so as a sort of defense against our own anxiety about the future. We face the enormous tasks of the postwar world, and so, if we can only draw up a plan that is symmetrically and logically consistent, we feel better, even if it is mostly fantasy and quite at variance with our cultural patterns.

My task this morning is to point out that Western European cultural traditions are in need of reconstruction as much as, if not more than, the social-economic practices through which they are so largely expressed.

Suppose we said to ourselves, "Hitler is only the most recent of a long line of similar individuals who have been produced by Western European culture. Each country has had someone whom it has called So-and-So the Great, who has been called great largely because of the way he has exploited or destroyed others. Instead of blaming individuals are we prepared to examine Western European cultural traditions as the source of the disorder, frustration of human values, and defeat of our aspirations? Are we prepared to see that our historically developed structure of ideas and beliefs, patterns of conduct and of selectively organized feelings, may itself produce the turmoil, confusion, almost continual war and destruction of European life, and that the cause is not merely the institutional patterns of government and economics, or perverse individuals? The international conflicts and the lack of internal social order may be only a symptom of a much deeper lying sickness or disorder—cultural disorder.

Have we the courage and the imagination to begin to do what the Greeks tried to do in the sixth and fifth centuries B.C., when they began to examine their tradition, to question the validity of their ideas and beliefs, to criticize their past and to try to reformulate equivalent conceptions and assumptions in terms of the new knowledge, the new insights that they were beginning to develop through their explorations?

That is the question that we must face when we begin to talk about cultural reorganization. I have ventured to put it before this group, because I believe that only in so far as we can reformulate our traditions, reformulate our basic assumptions and redefine our goals—only so far are we going to be able to preserve the values which we think most important.

Looking back, what have been the great occasions of human advance, particularly in Western European culture? Well, you may say, new ideas, new knowledge; but primarily, I think the decisive factor has been an extension of, or the rise of new, sensibilities where the basic value of human personality, the dignity of man, has been extended and given a new and larger meaning, applicable to other individuals. Look at the history of slavery and serfdom. Look at the treatment of women and children in the past. Any improvement came from a progressive extension of sensibilities. That is why I am personally convinced that the major resources we can use for cultural reconstruction are going to be the arts, because it has been through the arts that those sensibilities have been largely transmitted.

However, we ought to recognize how difficult it is to look at Western European culture, because it means looking at ourselves, our own pattern of life, our own pattern of thinking and acting and believing. You, as I, therefore, might wish to invite that mythical visitor from Mars, who would come to us free of the prejudices of American, Western European, or any other earthly culture. If we can imagine such a person, what would he tell us about the task of cultural reconstruction?

If he came and looked at us, the first thing he would say would be to give due recognition to the great achievement of Western European culture, the vision that has animated our prophets and our seers and our artists, all those who have helped to advance this great aspiration toward making a human way of life that has sought dignity and kindliness and worthwhileness. We can be proud of that achievement.

But then he would begin to ask us why we are not more aware of what a few people have already pointed out, namely, the progressive obsolescence of most of the basic assumptions of Western European culture—about the nature of the universe and how it operates, the relationship of man to that universe, the conception of the place of the individual in his society, the conception of human nature and the image of the self. All of those historic conceptions have become progressively incredible in the light of our new knowledge and understanding, our new criteria of credibility.[2]

I should like to venture here the assertion that there is no basic conflict between religion and science. The question is, What science are we going to utilize in our religious formulations and in the attempt to organize our lives and give basic dimensions to our culture? May we not say that our traditional religious formulations embodied the best science of the day of their formulation? Do we not need today to reformulate these assumptions and beliefs in terms of our new knowledge of the universe, the new, immense time perspective we now have on the world and on man? We could thereby perform for today a service comparable to what was performed by the great seers and prophets of the past, who labored to do that very task of utilizing the new knowledge and insights and sensibilities of their day to give the culture new dimensions and new formulations.

What science are we going to use? The science of ages ago or the on-going scientific work of today? You may say, "Suppose there is a difference between the formulations that we have revered and the new knowledge, what difference does it make?" It makes a tremendous difference, because those basic assumptions provide the dimensions of our values, and when those cultural formulations, which were once unquestioned and unquestionable, begin to lose their credibility and their authority, then something begins to happen to the personality of man; he becomes anxious, insecure, worried; he can no longer face life with security and sureness and hope.

Just look at what is happening today. Let me give you a concrete instance. We are trying to administer justice today in our courts by administration of the oath. I do not know how many of you have served on juries, but I am impressed, after many years' service on juries, with the number of people for whom the oath has no real

[2] See the writer's paper, "Science and Culture", *Scientific Monthly*, Vol. I, June, 1940.

significance. Juries no longer try to determine who is telling the truth. The question is, who is lying the least? There are people who still respect the oath, who have some personal integrity and some religious integrity, but, in general, I think we have a situation in trying to administer justice on the basis of the oath similar to what happened in the thirteenth century, before trial by jury came in, when justice was administered through trial by combat, which became progressively incredible and scandalously corrupt.

I could elaborate quite a number of ways in which progressive deterioration in the basic assumptions of Western European culture is showing itself in social disorder and in individual personality disintegration.

Any visitor from outside would be struck by what has happened in the centuries since Copernicus, Galileo, Newton and Kepler, and others who have systematically reformulated the older assumptions about the kind of universe, man's place therein, whence he came and what makes things happen. Just now we are going through perhaps one of the major shifts in the climate of opinion with the coming of relativity, field theory, and quantum physics—a revolution just as far-reaching as that which was ushered in by Copernicus and Galileo. We have hardly begun to realize what has so recently happened.

Our visitor would also begin to point out the internal incongruity and conflicts of our cultural traditions; the affirmation, the reiterated belief in the value of human personality, the assertion of the primary value of human dignity, and then all the contrary disruptive, destructive traditions and practices we also cherish in our religions and philosophies. Perhaps, if he thought he dared to do so—because I think we would like to have candor from our visitor—he would ask us whether we really believed in the dignity of man; whether we believed that man has any intrinsic worth and dignity other than that which is given him from outside sources, and he would remind us that man is constantly trying to validate himself by various achievements and destructive activities, because he has no belief in his own intrinsic integrity and worth.

Is not one of the major characteristics of Western European culture the extraordinary image of the self we have developed? Does not that give us a clue to the striving, the ambitious careering, the ruthless exploitation, the trying to establish one's self in the world in which one has no personal worth or place, despite our reiteration of man's human dignity as one of our major values? You see, as someone has pointed out, the knights were always talking about their valor and their virtue, but they were not very much convinced of it. They had to go around and reiterate it and revalidate it constantly to reassure themselves, and one wonders whether that is not the picture of Western European man, and whether it does not give a clue to what he does to his society and to other people; he has no real inner security, no inner integrity, and no feeling of personal worth except as he may be favored by divine power. He has "whatness" but not "whoness," as my friend, Dr. Plant, has so succinctly put it.

And would not our visitor point out to us how we have until very recently almost generally tried to socialize children by coercion, by humiliation, threatening, even terrorizing them into trying to make them sociable and law-abiding, as if they were really, as our traditions say, innately wicked and sinful or fallen from grace, and therefore we could not expect them to be decent and sociable unless we did something terrible to them. Is not that part of our tradition? Does that give us a clue to the kind of distorted human personalities we foster, that we ourselves are—we who find it so hard to maintain social order, to manifest and bring into realization the cultural values which are our dearest possessions.

Is it not curious that so many of the really decent human things are presented as Commandments, as dictates, as authoritative impositions which the individual must obey rather than as ways of feeling toward others—one human being toward another? Seriously, if you begin to reflect, is it not curious that we have to have a Commandment to "Honor thy father and thy mother"? Would any other culture do that? Do we know of any other cultures that command children under threat of supernatural sanction to "Honor thy father and thy mother"? Other cultures try to build a pattern of human relationships between parents and children where mutual respect and honor is a naive, almost impulsive way of acting and feeling. Are not those the questions we must begin to ask ourselves about our culture, if we are really consciously desirous of building the kind of orderly, humanly fulfilling life that we have always hoped for?

Are we perpetuating archaic patterns of socializing children in trying to create social order? Other cultures do not do that. They do not do these destructive things to their babies and children that we do. That is perfectly clear. They treat a child as one who will not stay if you do not give him a great deal of love and affection and make him feel that this is a hospitable world. Therefore, they treat children gently and with dignity. We do not do that. From the very start we say, "Look here, you are bad, wicked, worthless and you have to do this because I say so."

Should we not candidly examine what we are doing to the human personality, make a candid assay of Western European culture, and begin to recognize the immense human wastage of criminals and delinquents, the mentally disordered, the sex offenders, the neurotics, the ruthless power-driven individuals who spend their whole time in trying to get even for their past lives, trying to demonstrate they are not as bad nor as worthless as they were told in childhood? In all candor must we not agree with our visitor that we have a culture that does deplorable things to the human personality which are wholly incongruous and contradictory to our major ethical aspirations, but which are sanctioned by other traditional beliefs?

Can we go on asserting individual human worth and repeating the aspiration toward individual moral autonomy, unless we can find some way of rearing individuals so that they are emotionally capable of moral autonomy and individual responsibilities, and can help to maintain social order without this human wastage, this personality distortion, which we find so widespread? What kind of image of the self are we giving the individual who shows himself in these disorderly, destructive patterns of conduct?

We cannot take all the credit for our lofty ethical aspirations and great moral formulations without also taking the responsibility for all the failures. That is why I ask whether we can begin now to talk about a doctrine of individual responsibility which says the individual is responsible for everything he does, regardless of how he has been treated in childhood. Is it to be the great ethical advance of our generation and the generations to come, that they accept the doctrine of cultural responsibility the way our predecessors accepted and formulated the doctrine of individual responsibility? And if that is so, does it not lead one to an assay of all our institutions—business, industry, schools, religion and family—in terms of whether we are fostering the kinds of human beings who are capable of bearing the burdens of freedom, of being responsible, morally autonomous individuals? Is not that the kind of challenge which we have to face today, instead of continually denouncing people for failing to live up to the standards of conduct we cherish?

Do we not have to look at our Western European culture in terms of a question like this: Why do we find so many passively submissive individuals today and in the past, willing to be used by those in authority for destruction and defeat? Is it because our whole Western European culture has been based on the dominance-submission hierarchy all the way through, in our religion, our industry, our army, our political organization, and in our family life? Is that dominance-submission hierarchy of authority and control the best we can do to pattern human relationships and achieve our ethical aspirations? Is it compatible with the conception of human dignity and worth to ask individuals to abase themselves and proclaim their inferiority as we do in our social and religious beliefs? Or is that just one of the historically developed but now archaic beliefs which we can improve upon, just as we have improved upon so many others? Just think back over the record of how man has been humiliated and exploited and degraded and also inhumanly mistreated under the sanction of these beliefs.

It does not mean that we deny the past, that we repudiate our major values when we say that we should reformulate them and find equivalent practices, equivalent processes, that are less destructive and more consonant with our newer understandings and sensibilities. We have done that in every other area of life. Why is it that we have this belief that in the conduct of human relations there can be no further advance? Is not this one of the curious things about Western culture, that somehow we believe that once there has been a formulation, there can be no further advances or improvements thereon?

It does seem indeed curious. We have gone ahead in medicine, for example. We used to think in these terms about typhoid fever: here was a poor sick person, probably it was due to his own fault, punishment for his own wickedness or misdeeds. Then we developed an epidemiological viewpoint that typhoid fever could be regulated and eliminated by sanitary control of water and milk supplies.

I am trying to suggest that perhaps if we had a conception of cultural epidemiology we could begin to identify the persistent sources of the human destruction and disorder in our cultural traditions and customary ways of life. If Western European culture has been continuously warring, destructive and sadistic, we should candidly look at the record of man's inhumanity to man and the traditional ideas and beliefs which have been invoked as justification for such treatment. Can we go on reiterating our lofty ideals, our ethical formulations, without asking ourselves whether we are perpetuating ideal beliefs and practices which persistently defeat those aspirations?

Again, our visitor would point out that Western European culture is noteworthy in being obsessed by a fundamentally defeatist viewpoint in life; that in all our social theories and a large part of our religious formulations we are told that man cannot do anything about his difficulties and problems, he is helpless. For example, we are being told that war is a divine punishment for our wickedness and irreligion. It is curious to look at our theoretical statements about our economic and political life which tell us that we are at the mercy of these supposedly large-scale social forces which we must study as astronomers study the movement of the stars and then accommodate ourselves to their movements with resignation.

Is it not curious that these man-made historical institutions, such as the price system, occupy a position of superhuman coerciveness over human life? Why do we think of our economic practices as an all-powerful mechanism to which we must make human sacrifices? I think the only reason is that there is a tradition of man's helplessness, of his inability to meet the tasks of life with courage and with competence, based on the belief that man is a lowly, worthless creature except in so far as he is rescued by divine grace. Just look at the history of medicine; how many of the advances of medicine have been resisted or opposed, on the ground that they were interfering with divine ordinance.

Are we as helpless as our theories and our philosophy and our religious beliefs tell us? If so, where does that tradition come from? Is that one of the basic traditions in Western European culture that we ought to examine more critically? Can we formulate a new conception that man can create his own social life, because social life is his own creation and can be changed and directed and reorganized, if we have the courage, the imagination, and the sensibilities to do it?

It seems to me that that is the kind of question we should ask ourselves, particularly in view of the fact that if we do not, all the elaborate economic and political plans for postwar reconstruction upon which we are basing so much hope may prove vain. So much of postwar planning takes the form of elaborate organizations, regulations, and policing to compel people to be orderly and decent while the beliefs and practices which foster such behavior go on.

Our time is up. If time were available, I should like to point out quite a number of things on which we need a new time perspective to guide man from now on. We also have to think of building a human way of life for man as a part of world order, and of trying to make Western European culture come to terms with other historically developed cultures, many of which are older than ours and are cherished by their people just as much as we cherish ours, but in relation to which we have had something of a paranoiac conception that we are superior. As I have pointed out, Hitler has only stated the Western European paranoiac conception of superiority over other cultures, a little more brutally and destructively than many of us have felt toward other people.[3]

Is it not time that we were more candid and asked ourselves whether we have a monopoly on truth and a monopoly on all worthwhile ways of life, particularly when we recognize how much other cultures have created of beauty and significance and human dignity, and that they have created patterns of human relations some of which are superior to our own? Do we not need a little more candor and a little more courage to look at ourselves from that viewpoint? And then, do we not need, all of us who are concerned with this, to recognize that the more we praise the great figures, the seers, the prophets, the religious leaders in the past for what they have contributed, the more is the obligation upon us to try to do for our day what they did for their day?

That seems to be the only way that we can pay our debts to our cultural forebears and predecessors, and if we can face these persistent tasks of life with courage, with hope, and with a fundamental faith in human values, and utilize the knowledge and insights that are now available, then I think we can significantly advance man's search for those human values and for a social order and a world order that will offer some dignity, some significance, and some realization of the values that we cherish.

[3] Cf. the writer's paper "World Order and Cultural Diversity", *Free World,* Vol. III, No. I, June, 1942.

EDUCATION IN THE POSTWAR WORLD [1]

By

GEORGE S. COUNTS, Ph.D.

Professor of Education, Teachers College, Columbia University

The past twenty-five years have taught us that organized education may be a tremendous social force. The demonstration of its potency has not come from the democracies, but from the totalitarian powers, and particularly from the Soviet Union and Nazi Germany. The course of affairs in those countries can hardly be understood without reference to their educational program.

A visitor to Russia in the 'twenties was surprised and even amused at the avowed intention of the leaders to "change the character of the Russian people." They have not done that completely, of course, but they have wrought a tremendous transformation in the character of the people. Those Russians who stood before Stalingrad were not the Russians of the period from 1914 to 1917. Something had happened to them. Organized education played an enormous role in the transformation.

One would not have thought it possible in the 'twenties that the mentality of German youth could be molded into the present pattern. A Scottish scholar who lectured in this country in the 1830's remarked on certain evidences of antisemitism, which, he said, existed in most countries, but was conspicuously absent or negligible in Germany! This was probably true of Germany until after the First World War, but organized education in Nazi Germany has very successfully molded an antisemitic mental pattern. This illustrates the importance of education in developing attitudes which we

[1] Dr. Counts' lecture was summarized by the editor on the basis of the stenographic record.

count on in building the postwar world. A nation's educational program thus becomes a concern of all the nations.

What is education going to be like—what should it be like—after the war? On the assumption that we shall win the war and that an attempt will be made to build a durable peace, we can be reasonably sure of some things with reference to the quantitative phase of education. First, there will be an expansion of organized education. Not only is the realization of the importance of education increasing, but the economic situation will dictate an extension of the educational program. We shall have a most extraordinary occupational distribution—perhaps fifteen to twenty million people in the manufacturing and mechanical industries shifting to other occupations. Reemploying ten million young men and women demobilized from the armed services will involve a large problem of retraining. Furthermore, if unemployment is to be abolished, the lessened demand for labor in the production and distribution of material goods —due to the great advance of technology—will mean that large numbers of people will have to find employment in fields of personal service. Education is one of these services and may be expected to claim a share of this influx.

Pre-school education should have emphasis in this expansion. The churches have long recognized the importance of the period of early childhood, but recent psychological studies have freshly emphasized the significance of the first six years of life, in terms of personality, character, and the growth of intellectual powers. Society must cease to neglect this early period of life in its educational program.

Also we are likely to see an expansion of education at the youth level. A youth problem is anticipated at the end of the war. Experimentation will doubtless be carried on (not quite, perhaps, along the lines of the NYA and the CCC camps) and there will be a problem of inducting youth into working life. Adult education, too, will probably be considerably expanded.

But aside from these quantitative developments, there will be an expansion in the conception of education. Less and less will it be identified with schools and more and more with other institutions that educate. The school will doubtless continue to be the foremost educational agency, but voluntary, non-school agencies will play an increasing role. We may expect to see greater emphasis placed on the home, the church, clubs, recreation centers, travel, and other types of association.

More important, perhaps, for our consideration is the question, What has the generation now ending, which has witnessed two world wars, learned about education? Aside from the lesson of the great importance of education, three new emphases seem to emerge as we seek to answer this question: first, an appreciation of the technological revolution; secondly, a grand conception of our people; thirdly, a grand conception of our world. Each of these must find a place not hitherto accorded to it in the education of the future.

The great technological revolution which has changed the material basis of our society has had scant attention in the school curriculum. It has brought about the application of science to every department of life. It has transformed our economy, changing the modes of production and exchange. One does not have to go all the way with the Marxists in their economic determinism to recognize the basic importance in the culture of the modes of production and exchange.

This revolution has changed the contours of society, producing a vaster integration. It has furnished the basis of a world community. The maxim of Hitler's school of geopolitics that the world has become a small neighborhood, is true. From the standpoint of the factors that bring communities into relationship, the earth is today no larger, perhaps, than the Thirteen Colonies at the time this Republic was founded.

Again, technology has changed the modes of government and of warfare. New agencies of communication have come into being, and the power to control the human mind has been greatly extended. New engines of warfare, coupled with the contraction of the world, have given the present war a peculiarly decisive character. It has become possible for a despot to rule the earth as easily as he could rule a small state in the eighteenth century.

These are major aspects of the impact of technology upon our life which give importance to the technological revolution as subject matter for education. From the earliest years up to the university level, materials should be introduced into the curriculum designed systematically to introduce the young to all aspects of this revolution, so that they may understand its origin, its spread over the world, and its social consequences. The methods and instruments of science, technological processes, and the natural resources they develop, mechanical power and the chemistry and metallurgy involved in it, the organization of labor, the whole complex of production and distribution—all these should find their way into the education of youth.

This will involve new instrumentalities and methods. The school shop and laboratory will not be sufficient. There must be intimate contact with the life of the community. Peter Drucker in *The Future of Industrial Man* (John Day Co.) says: "That so many children have never seen a cow is generally regarded as a scandal—and rightly so. But that a great many more—especially in Europe—have never been inside a factory should have been even more astounding." He is quite right. The exploitation of children in the early days of the Industrial Revolution led to legal prohibitions against their employment in factories. Yet work experience has always been among the most important educative experiences. Children now grow up in industrial communities without any close contact with the processes by which people gain their livelihood.[2]

No doubt, a difficult problem is involved here, because of the sharp distinction between "public" and "private," as applied respectively to the schools and to industrial enterprise. But a way must be found to furnish this fundamental education in the nature and results of the technological revolution. The American people have contributed more to it than any other people, excepting, perhaps, the English. Yet they have not seen its implications. The Nazis, the Communists, and the Japanese military caste have understood it better than the leaders of democratic societies.

In 1925 the lecturer drew up a list of forty-five occupations and asked senior high-school students in different parts of the country to rate them from the point of view of their standing in the community. The ratings were almost identical for all sections of the

[2] There is no intention here, of course, to belittle the importance of protective legislation.

country. Who their parents were, what their own prospects were, made no difference in these youngsters' ranking of the occupations. The experiment was repeated in Russia the following summer with children of the same ages. In the Russian rankings the three highest were aviator, civil engineer, and machinist, in that order, each of which was rated low by the American students. The Russian youth had learned the meaning of the technological revolution.

The second major emphasis in postwar education should be the development of a great and grand conception of our people—of their past and of their future. If the question should be asked what has been the major weakness of American education, the answer might well be that it has been a moral weakness. We have a good educational system but not a great one. We have talked much about democracy but have not made a very serious attempt to translate our words into the life and work of the schools. Perhaps the greatest challenge of our time is to develop a conception of the American people that will give moral and social direction to our educational program. We are challenged at this point by the totalitarian states. They developed a great conception of their people. The Nazi conception is a terrible one but it is great in its potency. The Russians created a great conception of Russia, its revolution, its future, and its role in world history.

Can we produce a conception of America and American life that will meet the totalitarian challenge? It is doubtful if our democracy will survive without that. And it is in our democratic heritage that the source of such a great conception is to be found. That heritage has various roots. In part it comes from the Judaic-Christian tradition, with its affirmation of the worth and dignity of the individual, the brotherhood of man and the equality of all races and peoples, and its emphasis on the quality of mercy—the idea that the strong should show mercy to the weak.

From the ancient Greeks comes faith in the human mind and in the powers of man. From the Anglo-Saxons we have derived a great love of political liberty. And as our own contribution to this democratic heritage there is that fierce assertion of social equality that developed on the frontier and in our early agrarian society. Imperfect as is our application of the principle of social equality, we as a people hold to it tenaciously.

A further enrichment of our democratic heritage comes from the working people's movement of the last hundred years or so, with its demand for economic justice. The old economic foundation of democracy—the land—no longer serves. A new one may be found in the right to work. The working people, with their trade union movement and their stimulus to radical social thinking, have given us a greater understanding of the economic basis of human liberty.

Finally, technology itself has contributed to our democratic heritage, for it holds out the promise of a great alleviation of the bitter struggle for livelihood out of which come wars and class conflicts. Technology makes possible the abolition of physical privation, misery, and starvation. It is strange indeed that it should take a war to demonstrate the capacity of our economy—an income production of perhaps 150 billion, whereas in 1929 it was 80 billion or so.

Dr. Charles A. Beard has related that when he finished college he went to Europe to study—to England, France, and Germany. As he studied he became ashamed of his own people because American history seemed so thin, so meager, as compared with the history of the European peoples. Then he returned to America, took a chair at Columbia University, began to restudy American history, and changed his mind. It was not our history that was thin, but the work of the historians. It was a rich history, he decided, the record of which has still to be written. It is the story of the struggle of refugees from Europe, underprivileged and exploited folk, who rose from virtual slavery to become free men and women. And they are still on their way. In this rich past and in the future that beckons, are the elements of the great conception of our people that education must give to the youth of America.

The third emphasis, which can only be briefly mentioned here, is a new conception of the world we live in, a world that has become a potential neighborhood in which many races and peoples dwell. In it they must learn to live together. Americans have lived so long in isolation between two great oceans that they have the illusion of a possible independent existence. The young must learn that this is not possible. They must have a grand conception of their world, a world now in the making. And they must be equipped to bear the heavy responsibility that will rest on their generation to build this new world.

RECONSTRUCTION IN INTERNATIONAL LAW

By

CLYDE EAGLETON, PH.D.

Professor of International Law, New York University

The first state constitution of Massachusetts in a famous quotation tells us that it was written "to the end that this may be a government of laws and not of men." The purpose of the United Nations, if we may believe the Atlantic Charter and the utterances of their statesmen, is to build an international system of law, and not of Hitlers.

If we are to build this better world of law, we must devote a great deal of attention to the law of nations. That law has been in disrepute for some time. It has been the butt of witticisms, and the object of ridicule and scorn. Many of the scoffers were merely irresponsible persons, for whom a law governing nations was too far away to be within the realm of cognition; others were cynics or pessimists who regarded it as beyond realism and practicality to think of bringing sovereign states under a rule of law; others put their trust in nationalism and patriotism, refused to submit their nation to the "rule of furriners" and preferred instead to risk economic ruin and the anarchy of war and power politics. There are others, however, in the profession of law itself, to whom I address a paragraph of especial recrimination. Some in that profession—and they were formerly more numerous than now—tell us that law is derived solely from the facts of practice; that it grows in its own way, and that we cannot and should not attempt to shape its growth. Toward the beginning of the present war, at a meeting of the American Society of International Law, a distinguished member gently derided "those gentlemen of the theological school" in the Society who "postulate a kind of natural law and condemn positive law." Others suggested that the anxious words of some of us, calling for support for the law of nations, were wasted energy, since the law ultimately prevails regardless of human influence. To me, no theory is more impotent, more deadening, than that which teaches us that law "just grows," that it needs no human assistance, that the efforts and beliefs of man have no part in its making. One does not have to deny that custom is a substantial part of law, or dispute that law is a social growth, to say that law cannot grow or stand alone. Law is a human institution, and it depends upon human support.

I was glad to find support of this belief in the opening words of the Preliminary Recommendation of the Inter-American Juridical Committee, which after noting the abandonment by positivists of the moral basis of law recognized by Grotius and others, goes on to say of positivist writers that "they abandoned almost entirely the task of formulating moral standards by which the conduct of nations might be judged, and instead they adopted the pragmatic standard that the actual practice of nations, as expressed in usages and customs, constituted the only valid international law. The result was that the exponents of this mistaken theory came to determine the existence of rules of international law by the record of the conduct of nations, instead of judging the conduct of nations by the principles of law."

However, it is not my purpose to lament the sad past or to enter into controversies of legal philosophy. The need today is for action, not for dialectics, and I do not propose to waste time in discussing the positivist, or functional, or sociological or any other theoretical approach to international law. Those who have been witty and scornful in the past now realize that the law which they scorned was their own law, and that the sad state of the world today is a direct consequence of their neglect of that law in the past. While they are in this mood, while the problem of reconstruction is thrust upon us all, let us not lament or theorize, but ask what should be done. How has international law failed in the past and what are its needs for the future? If it requires human support, in what respects does it need it?

In the past, international law has been defective: first, in that it did not cover important fields of international intercourse; secondly, in that there was no adequate procedure for making new law or changing the old law; thirdly, in that there was no adequate procedure for upholding such law as there was; and finally, it lacked moral foundation and moral support.

I. One of the chief, if not the very first, of the purposes of law anywhere is the restraint of violence; yet international law has not been permitted to declare that the use of force by its subjects is illegal. Law and force are antithetical elements, yet international law was compelled to accept the theory that force, even when used to override the law, was not illegal. It was a ridiculous situation, worthy of scorn; but the scorn does not belong to the law. It must be credited to those persons who claimed for their own nations the right to use force; who put national sovereignty and patriotism above international law and order. A domestic lawyer who would regard as an outlaw any person who set his individual liberty above law, might—and some still do—encourage his nation to assert that its sovereignty was above that of the law of nations. Law is impotent, when force is its master, rather than its servant.

The inability to control the use of force was and is the greatest defect of international law; but there are other fields also in which it has been permitted little or no sway. Economic nationalism has been a form of warfare almost as much in need of control as military warfare. In this field, national groups have sought to advance their own interests at the expense of others through selfish and arbitrary use of national power. In the field of social welfare also, and of human rights in general, the law of nations has been permitted little voice.

II. One of the reasons, doubtless, why international law has been so confined in its range of jurisdiction is the procedural difficulty of making new law. It is usually said that the sources of international law are custom, treaty, and the general principles of law; of these, only the treaty can be useful in the process of legislation. But the treaty is a quite inadequate process for making law; it was never intended for this purpose, though quite a respectable number of legislative treaties have been included in the Treaty Series of the League of Nations during the past two decades. The trouble with these treaties is that they are not of general application; each is limited to those states which have ratified it, for no sovereign state could be bound to such legislation without its own consent. It is not an easy thing to make law when the process requires the consent of every subject of the law; yet this is the way by which international legislation has been accomplished. Not much progress can be expected so long as the consent of those who are opposed to progress must be obtained.

It is as important to change old law as it is to make new law. The paradoxical result of the unwillingness of states to be bound by any change without their own consent was to make war the only way in which a treaty could be changed without the consent of all the signatories thereto. For war was not illegal, and its results were legal, even though they might override a treaty. This anomaly was not unknown to international lawyers, but there was little they could do about it. *Pacta sunt servanda*—treaties must be obeyed—was, of course, a fundamental rule; but it could sometimes work injustice. Therefore, said some of the publicists, *pacta sunt servanda, rebus sic stantibus*—the treaty was valid so long as the presumably fair conditions under which it was made remained unchanged. But if conditions had changed, with resultant injustice, then the treaty was not binding. There is theoretical strength in this argument; but the practical difficulty is that each state is its own judge as to whether conditions have so changed as to invalidate its obligation under the treaty. Japan could claim that treaties restricting her plans were no longer binding upon her; and there was no way by which her claim, backed by force, could be denied. Not until there is a community judge to whom the question must be submitted can such a principle be accepted. The whole process of "peaceful change," the necessary development of progress and justice without resort to violence, is bound up in this difficulty; and no more important need exists in the community of nations than a legislative process through which such change can be achieved. The theory of consent, now destroyed as a theory, but still practiced by states, must be overruled; if we are to have justice and order in the community of nations, there must be times when a state which has refused to approve a new law must nevertheless be bound by it.

III. The law of nations, though it has had no policeman behind it, has been remarkably well observed in the past; it has probably been as well obeyed as domestic law. Possibly this was due to its lack of jurisdiction in important fields of conflict. But, even within its limited field, even in the law of peace, everything could be upset by the interference of war, itself as legal as the law which it upsets. Even the threat of war, or the necessity of preparing for war, leads states to disregard their legal obligations, and even more inclines them against accepting new obligations. I shall return to this in a moment.

For the situations in which the law is violated, no sufficient sanction is provided. There is no policeman who can bring an offender to court, or compel the observance of a treaty. There is no general obligation upon states to submit to the compulsory jurisdiction of a court, though great advance has been made through the voluntary acceptance by many states of such an obligation in various fields. The American nation has thus far refused to submit to compulsory adjudication of its disputes.

IV. Law, I repeat, is a human institution, and if it fails, human beings have failed. In a democracy, such as the United States, the responsibility for the failure of international law lies at the door of each citizen, personally. The observation has often been made that a person who governs his own conduct by a strict moral code, nevertheless urges upon his nation an immoral code, and encourages it in acts of lawlessness, of deceit and dishonesty, of robbery and murder. The average American would indignantly deny such an imputation, but he must nevertheless be held guilty; he has not applied or upheld in international affairs the moral principles which he upholds in other relationships. He has not given to international law the moral foundation without which no system of law can prevail.

For this failure to inculcate a proper moral conduct between peoples, the churches must accept a large share of responsibility. The Protestant churches have been divided, stumbling and uncertain, and shamefully weak in their support of right against wrong in international affairs. The Catholic Church has been dogmatic and, until recently, uncooperative. The Jewish group, so far as my observation goes, has been concerned only with special fields such as the protection of the rights of minorities. All, I am happy to say, are now awake and beginning to work valiantly together in support of international law and order, where their cause is necessarily a common cause.

In a recent issue of the *New York Times,* on adjoining pages, were messages from Pope Pius XII and from the American Institute of Judaism. The Pope, in his Christmas address, said: "That social life, as God willed it, may attain its scope, it needs a juridical order to support it from without" and then continued: "Any one who considers with an open and penetrating mind the vital connection between social order and a genuine juridical order will realize at once the urgent need of a return to a conception of law which is spiritual and ethical, serious and profound, vivified by the warmth of true humanity and illumined by the splendor of the Christian faith which bids us seek in the juridical order an outward refraction of the social order willed by God, a luminous product of the spirit of man which is in turn the image of the spirit of God." And, on the next page, the Institute of Judaism asserted that "this time in which we live may be the acid test of religious sincerity. Unless all religions eschew sectarianism and learn to unite upon their essentials, unless they make a valiant and wholehearted effort to interpret their beliefs in terms of social action, they may well forfeit their right to the allegiance of men."

The Federal Council of the Churches of Christ, at its Delaware Conference in March, 1942, adopted as the first in its Statement of Guiding Principles: "We believe that moral law, no less than physical law, undergirds our world. There is a moral order which is fundamental and eternal, and which is relevant to the corporate life of men and the ordering of human society. If mankind is to escape chaos and recurrent war, social and political institutions must be brought into conformity with this moral order."

Not merely religious groups assert the need of a moral code to undergird the law of nations. From the Preliminary Report of the Commission to Study the Organization of Peace, I quote a sentence: "No system of laws and organization can be of value without the living faith and spirit behind and in it. . . . Our problem is largely an ethical one; it involves . . . a belief in the existence of a power in the world that makes for righteousness." I have already quoted from the Inter-American Juridical Committee a paragraph which reveals its belief in the moral foundation of law.

I have not quoted these statements because I am speaking in a theological seminary, but because of my own firm conviction that international law must have a more solid foundation than whatever the prevailing practice of states is at a given moment. It must have a moral foundation. There are certain moral principles which can be accepted by all peoples, regardless of politics or religion; without agreement upon these, and sincere support for them by individuals everywhere, there can be no hope for the reconstruction of international law. It is to the churches, chiefly, who can reach the people with this lesson—if the churches can first agree—that we must look for the accomplishment of this task. I have more hope now that the churches will succeed at this than I had a year ago.

I have been talking about the defects of international law, not by way of lamentation, but to discover what is wrong and what repairs or remedies will be needed. Law is usually the result of the pressure of conflicts between human beings who are, in the long run, reasonable; and who, when they are forced to it, will submit to a rule of law rather than engage in interminable fighting. We like to think of ourselves as intelligent persons, who anticipate need and sit down together to prepare laws in advance of conflict; but the fact is that we are negligent and unwilling, and that we refuse to make the laws which we need until we are hurt. It is danger, or actual suffering which, ordinarily, induce us to accept new law; and this situation confronts us in the international field today. The tragic failures and the continuous conflict of the past two or three decades, the economic depression and wars, have shocked most of us into admitting that some submission of our patriotism and national sovereignty to an international law is essential.

There is, then, a more receptive atmosphere throughout the world to proposals for the reconstruction of international law. The need for such law is now more widely recognized; and so much of the old law has been wrecked that it must be rebuilt as a whole. The effect of war is to weaken or destroy prejudices and vested interests; the psychology of the joint effort in which we are engaged encourages the adoption of new ideas.

It seems possible now to obtain the popular support which has for so long failed the law of nations, and which must be obtained in democracies before their governments can agree with other governments upon such law. It is worthy of repeated emphasis that the fault for the failure of international law rests upon individual citizens, and that the only hope for rebuilding it lies in their sincere support. Lip-service by the democracies has not been enough. While supporting the law of nations in noble words and even by observance of obligations, they have led to its collapse through unwillingness to accept the responsibility and the sacrifices necessary to make it effective. If the people of the democracies are now in a mood to admit past mistakes, they should rebuild the law of nations at once; otherwise, we shall emerge from this war into a situation in which there is no law, and each nation must strengthen itself for its own defense in whatever way seems possible. Present realization must not be nibbled away and dissipated by another Henry Cabot Lodge, who points out to the people trivial sacrifices which they must make, who appeals to petty prejudices, and who conceals from them what they have to gain. The American people, as well as others, must be informed as to the things which they must give up, and above all, must be shown what the gains for them will be. Let the balance sheet of loss from international anarchy and of gain through law and order be presented clearly to them, so that they will not be falsely disillusioned as they were in 1919.

What sort of law of nations must we build? To answer this, we must ask what changes have taken place in the world which made the old law and procedure ineffective; what pressures are at work to which nations must adapt themselves; what dangers confront us which we must guard against?

The leaven which has been chiefly at work during the past century or more, changing all our habits of life and producing other forces to which adjustment must be made, is the interdependence between human beings generated by the Industrial Revolution, and accumulating through technological advance and industrialization until it produced the crisis in which we now find ourselves. Before the effects of this change were felt, an individual could feel sure that, with ability and energy, he would be able to make his way in the world. Today, he can produce nothing for himself; he depends upon others for everything; and he does not even know who these others are. He is caught in a system which has grown up about him, and he cannot even be sure of making a living unless the system works efficiently. In this situation, he has been forced to call more and more upon government for protection and support, and the range of government within each nation has increased enormously.

In the community of nations, national sovereignty corresponds to individual liberty, and it likewise has been curtailed by the increasing interdependence of the peoples of the world. The process has naturally been slower as between nations, but the people know now that a nation can no more be self-sufficing and independent than an individual. Interdependence is an irresistible force, whether within or between nations. We have been adjusting ourselves to it slowly in domestic affairs, though without sufficient recognition of what must be done; but we have been far too slow in adjusting national sovereignty to this pressure. Whether between individuals or between nations, interdependence requires the same answer—more law and more organization.

This need has indeed been known, and efforts have been made to extend international law and organization; but, as we have seen, with little success. There now enters a new and terrible force, which not only makes further advance impossible, but will render ineffective such international law as remains. This is war—war in its modern character. War, too, has been changed by interdependence and technological advance; it has become so menacing and so costly and so pervasive that it will shape all human activities in the future, unless it can be brought under control. I do not have time properly to describe this change, for it is the most potent of the forces which are at work. Modern war lets no one escape. It puts to work, and consequently subjects to attack, every man, woman, and child; it is no longer possible to distinguish between civilians and combatants. It makes use of every conceivable thing; it is no longer possible to protect some private property in land warfare, or under the law of contraband and blockade in sea warfare. This sort of war does not stay within the bounds of belligerent territory, but spills out over the whole world; no people can be neutral, and the whole international law of neutrality is obsolete. It consumes for its weapons and tools all materials; and to produce the vast quantities required, the whole economic life of a nation must be organized under a strong central control. It diverts all human energies and all natural resources from the advancement of human welfare, and organizes them all for the destruction of human welfare.

Now, it is most important to realize that this situation will not end when the war ends, for the totalitarian regime necessary to fight a war must be continued in order to be ready for the next war. It takes years to become so organized that we can fight a modern war; and it is impossible from either a military or an economic viewpoint to be shifting our economic system from a war to a peace basis every time that some other state begins to produce a few more planes and tanks than we do. In this situation, we can no longer think of a period of peace, within which we can devote our energies to the things we wish to do. So long as the threat of war exists, we must remain organized for war, unable to advance human welfare; and no state can accept legal restrictions, or engage in international cooperation, for each must be strong and self-sufficient against the next war. To be prepared for this kind of war, a nation must make itself independent of anything outside it; it is compelled toward autarchy; no state can accept a law which might interfere with its ability to survive the next war. On the contrary, in order to be prepared, a state would not only make exclusive use of all its own resources, but reach out to seize from others what it might need. Modern war is not merely an occasional interruption of international law; it makes international law or cooperation impossible. If international law is to survive at all, it must be made strong enough to bring war under its control.

The result of the two forces above mentioned is to reduce the individual human being to a feeling of great insecurity, and thereby to produce another great pressure which will necessarily shape the building of the future. No human being today can feel secure against economic distress; no one can feel secure against the physical danger of war. Everywhere people are frightened; and this fear and discontent create a demand which will be overwhelming for protection against these dangers. Now, this human being is the unit of all social organization; by him, and for him, the state and all other human institutions have been created. For centuries, he has thought of the state as the highest form of organization, sufficient for all his purposes; but he is now realizing that the state is no longer adequate, under the changed circumstances of life, to give him the protection and assistance which he must have. He will, inevitably, look beyond the state; he will be increasingly interested in international law and government, for only by that law and by that power can his state be enabled to care for him as he desires. We may expect to find him demanding, with irresistible force, a regulation of international trade and intercourse under which he can find economic security, and a regulation of war which can give him security against this danger to his person and interests. Very probably, he will demand some international guarantees of his rights as a human being, not only because these rights are precious to him, but also because the international system upon which he is coming to rely cannot survive if within each state a Hitler can limit freedom of information and discussion and turn his people toward war.

International law, in the past, has dealt only with sovereign states, and to give it jurisdiction over individuals would be something of a revolution, and would produce many difficulties in theory and procedure. There is no doubt that the nation state will remain the political unit of society, and no doubt that it will continue to control most of the relations and activities of individuals; but it is much to be doubted whether the sovereign state can in the future claim so exclusive a jurisdiction over persons within its territory as was asserted for it by Chief Justice Marshall in the famous case of the Schooner Exchange. Whether through the state or in spite of the state, international law in the future will have to adapt itself to the needs of individuals, for it depends upon those individuals for its support.

If we put together the weaknesses of international law in the past, and the changes and pressures which will affect it in the future, we arrive unavoidably at the conclusion that further advance for international law, or even maintenance of its past position, is impossible without an organized international government. Interdependence necessitates more rules of law, particularly in the economic field; it requires also administrative organizations. This need has been recognized, and a number of international organizations have developed in the past, ranging from the Universal Postal Union or the Iceberg Patrol to the League of Nations. Such development, however, has been wrecked by war which, in its modern form, is not an occasional interruption of the legal order, but a continuing impediment. The first function of law is to restrain violence; and a legal system within which the use of force, even against itself, is not illegitimate, is impotent and useless. Force must be subjected to law and used only by law; and this authority can be given to international law only by the combined strength of all nations against the lawbreaker. No nation can be permitted again the immoral status of neutrality; it must be the duty of all to uphold the law.

But it is not enough, and not possible, to deprive a state of its right to use force, if force is the only method by which that state can remedy its wrongs and obtain justice for its people. Unless the community provides justice, as well as peace, no state will submit to a law against war. Consequently, means for making and changing international law, through community action, must also be provided, strong enough to prevail over the veto of an interested state. Clearly, too, there must be compulsory submission of disputes to a community tribunal. To demand an international police against aggressors is to demand a complete system of international government.

This international order must, in order to meet the needs and demands of human beings everywhere, pay much less attention to national sovereignty, and much more attention to the dignity and welfare of the individual. This is not to say that the nation state must disappear; it is not even to suggest that its powers will be much diminished. But both national and international governments must work together for the social advance and economic security of individuals, and neither can do the job without the other.

The pressure of the forces above described, the changes in human life which have occurred, the insecurity of individuals everywhere —these things make necessary long steps of advance. The reconstruction of international law is possible only through the establishment of a strong international government. The dilemma has by now become inescapable. Unless we rebuild and extend the law of nations, and back it by powerful government, we can look forward to the destruction of humanity through the war which it refuses to control.

LABOR IN THE POSTWAR WORLD

By

JOHN A. FITCH, Ll.D.

Director of Industrial Courses,
New York School of Social Work, Columbia University

When the present war comes to an end with a victory of the United Nations over the Axis powers, labor will find itself confronted with new and difficult problems. To an equal degree they will be social problems, since they will affect the welfare of the entire fabric of society. Among the questions that will have to be dealt with will be those arising out of the unsettled and possibly chaotic conditions in industry attendant upon the transfer from a wartime to a peacetime economy; the difficulty that several million young men will encounter in making that same adjustment; the problem of providing job training to these millions, many of whom will have had no previous preparation for any job except that of soldier; the new position of women who have entered industry and will thus be competitors for employment at the very time when industry is in an unsettled state and demobilized soldiers are looking for work.

Other problems that will tax our ingenuity and statesmanship are indicated now in the outcry in some quarters for a complete relaxation of government control over business at the end of the war—a cry reminiscent of the Harding slogan in 1920 of "back to normalcy;" and in the rising demand for the curbing of union activity—the real nature of which is apparent in view of the patriotic record of organized labor in this war. Only once since such figures have been compiled in the United States has the record of man-days lost been as low as in 1942. There have been no strikes authorized by national unions since the beginning of January, 1942, and there has not been a single month, according to the War Labor Board, "in which the man-days lost from war production by strikes were greater than one-tenth of one per cent." [1]

Though we must begin now to prepare to meet these problems, we cannot deal with all of them here. Instead of attempting to do so, I propose to limit myself to the consideration of a few basic concepts, the acceptance of which will, in my opinion, make our adjustment to postwar conditions less difficult. In order to make the most of the time available I shall offer these concepts in the form of more or less dogmatic assertions.

First, then, labor is entitled to a living wage. Whatever may be true of particular individuals, I take it to be a self-evident proposition that labor, in the mass, is capable of earning and does earn a living. To put it another way, the effort put forth by economic society, including labor, has been sufficient over the years, and is currently sufficient to create the stock of goods and services essential to the maintenance of life. It has, as a matter of fact, done much better than that. Not only has production been sufficient to enable the human race to maintain its numbers—it has been so great that the population of the world has more than doubled in the past one hundred years.

The case is stated for Great Britain by Sir William Beveridge in his famous report on "Social Insurance and Allied Services." Surveys made in industrial centers in Britain between 1928 and 1937, says Sir William, "show that the total resources of the community were sufficient to make want needless . . . [and it] could have been abolished . . . by a redistribution of income; . . . [it] was a needless scandal due to not taking the trouble to prevent it." Before the beginning of the present war, "Abolition of want was easily within the resources of the community."

Evidence such as this reveals that labor produces enough goods to make the living wage possible, and is therefore entitled to have it. The term as I use it is not limited to an income merely while at work. Men do not live by work periods alone, nor by years alone, but by the lifetime. It is no living wage that does not provide in-

[1] This lecture was delivered on January 26, 1943.

come for the whole of the normal life, including the unproductive periods at the beginning and at the end. Nor is it a living wage if it does not provide purchasing power during interruptions in opportunity to earn during the middle period of normal working capacity. A living wage is that which enables the earner to meet all the natural exigencies of life, whatever they are, during a period that stretches, as the President has recently put it, "from the cradle to the grave." And since enough goods are produced to make this possible, it is obvious that labor earns such a wage whether particular workers get it in their pay envelopes or not.

But a living wage—or any wage—is possible only if one has a job. Much that is misleading has been said about the "right to work." Such a right is nothing more than a myth so long as it depends upon the willingness or ability of another to provide employment. As a matter of fact it is absence of the right to a job which, more than anything else, characterizes the status of labor in a free society. Here we are confronted with a singular paradox. If a wage earner is to obtain a living on terms that are acceptable either to himself or to society, he must work, yet the very practice and structure of society itself may at any given time deny him that opportunity. This creates a situation that is unethical and economically unsound. During a prolonged period of unemployment it leads to a system of relief under which the victim of this maladjustment is obliged to accept meager support at the hands of others. Instead of permitting the able bodied to do the work that is necessary to provide themselves with food, our society permits them to remain idle while others carry the double burden of providing food for themselves and for the unemployed as well. In any acceptable form of society the right to work for the necessities of life must be established and maintained.

In the third place, society must provide the worker with education. His own situation requires it and the welfare of society demands it. If the worker is to be guaranteed a job at a living wage he must somehow receive appropriate occupational training. And if he is to play an adequate role as a member of society he must have cultural training as well.

It is important to note that our present system of free education does not meet the foregoing requirements. This is true not only because of badly conceived school systems which are not adjusted to all community needs, and not alone because of absence of facilities in many areas due to lack of sufficient tax revenue. Education is not free to the boy or girl who because of poverty is obliged to leave school before receiving adequate training. As Justice Frankfurter has recently said, "To deny young people opportunity to equip themselves for their places in society merely because their parents lack financial resources, or for any other irrelevant circumstance, is to deny democracy itself. For it means nothing less than the denial to a democracy of the adequate use of its talents."

A fourth essential for labor is the full enjoyment of the rights inherent in a democratic society. There are gaps in the enforcement of the Bill of Rights and where this is the case, labor is apt to be affected. Freedom for unpopular opinion, particularly in the area of economic radicalism, is still to be fully achieved in the United States. In eight states the right to vote is made contingent on the payment of a poll tax. In a large section of the country Negroes are generally prevented from voting whether taxpayers or not. The sheer cost of obtaining justice is frequently a barrier to the assertion of rights.

These, then, are some of the essentials for American labor: a living wage, the right to work, free education, the full enjoyment of civil rights. What steps have been taken or can be taken to make these essentials living realities?

The living wage, as here defined, is still a dream, but there are forces at work toward that objective. Organized labor, of course, is attempting to attain economic security for its members, but there are very interesting tendencies to be observed in the field of legislation. Minimum wage laws in most of the leading industrial states do not require the payment of a living wage as here defined. Far from it! But they do establish the principle that society has an interest in the matter and that it is competent for the state to indicate the point below which wages will not be permitted to fall. Superimposed on the state laws is the federal Fair Labor Standards Act which provides a minimum wage for workers in interstate commerce. These laws, in the main, afford protection only to persons actually at work. A further step has been taken in New York where several industries, notorious for the irregularity of their requirements, have been required to obligate themselves for three days pay in any week in which workers are called for duty, thus abolishing the cat-and-mouse procedure of unrestrained dismissals after a single day of work. The New York Court of Appeals has affirmed the validity of this ruling.

Minimum wage requirements are effectively supplemented by the social security laws, which guarantee a limited income in case of work interruptions and in old age. Accident compensation is a statutory right in forty-seven states; unemployment compensation is paid in every state and old age benefits are provided for the country as a whole by federal statute. These laws are of limited application and the benefits are less than they should be. Furthermore, no provision is made for compensation in case of illness, nor for accidents or other disabilities occurring outside employment. But again the possibilities inherent in such legislation are very great. They are steps in the direction of a living wage because they provide income during periods when the worker is off the employer's payroll and they guarantee an income for life after age sixty-five in all cases, as of right, and without any inquiry as to need.

The "right to work," as stated before, is largely a myth. Yet there are two discernible forces which seem to be working toward a recognition, or a qualified recognition, of such a right. One such force is to be found in certain legal enactments. The National Labor Relations Act forbids the discharge of a worker because of union membership. If the employer does discharge for that reason, he may be required to reinstate the worker with pay for time lost. This is a definite limitation on the absolute freedom in hiring and firing that existed before the passage of the law.

The social security laws provide another example. The principle is embodied to some extent in all forms of social insurance, but it stands out most clearly in unemployment compensation. The very fact that these laws are generally designated, in this country at least, as unemployment compensation rather than as unemployment insurance laws reveals the underlying purpose. Compensation for what? All forms of social insurance contemplate payment of compensation for the suffering of some injury. The worker is compensated for accident or illness, or other forms of disability. In the case of unemployment the injury sustained is clearly and solely the loss of a job. By a money payment we compensate the worker for that loss.

The payment of indemnity to one who has suffered a property loss by reason of the act of another is an old and established principle. We are now extending that principle to cover the loss of employment. This does not establish a property right in the sense that the job may be positively held against other claimants, nor does the compensation paid under our present laws cover the monetary loss sustained. But when a thing possessed is recognized as having such importance to the individual that loss of it entitles the possessor to indemnity, it is difficult to avoid the inference that something approaching a property right is involved.

The other force working toward recognition of a property right in a job is organized labor. Through the medium of collective bargaining and the trade agreement, the unions attempt to establish a measure of job security. Two trade union officials, Clinton Golden and Harold Ruttenberg, have recently dealt with this matter in their book, *The Dynamics of Industrial Democracy* (Harper & Brothers). In discussing the principle of seniority in employment the authors say: "The unions have introduced a new doctrine into American industry (accepted for many years by British industry); namely, once management has hired an employee who makes good, except under agreed-upon circumstances, it must continue to give employment, or preference for employment, to that employee until such time, if ever, as he chooses to quit his job. Thus under union-management relations, governed by collective bargaining contracts, workers acquire a qualified property interest in their jobs—which they seek to make as inviolate as the most sacred interests of real-estate property."

Labor is still a long way from the status implied by this statement of principle. It is difficult to see, moreover, how a worker could ever obtain a right to a job that could approach the degree of inalienability that attaches to a property right. The opposite extreme, however—total absence of any claim to a job—is intolerable in a society that is either ethically minded or even intelligently aware of its own best interests. A greater degree of governmental concern about this whole matter is clearly indicated. The social insurance laws must be extended and liberalized, and the state must assume further and more positive responsibility for providing opportunities for employment.

With respect to education, I believe that the differences in opportunity now made inevitable by what Justice Frankfurter called the "irrelevant circumstance" of the parents' lack of financial resources, must be removed. This is not an easy task. It implies making available to the youth of the land the amount and kind of education it is able effectively to absorb. It means not only free text books and free tuition, but maintenance as well. Only thus will the potentialities of the youth of America achieve full development.

This idea is neither original nor new. Writing in *The New Republic* for January 25, 1943, Alexander Meiklejohn proposed that after the war the federal government should provide tuition and maintenance for all men discharged from the army, to enable them to complete their education. Early in the past century Thomas Jefferson was proposing common schools for all and a college education at public expense for exceptionally gifted students. The idea is reasonable and possible, but unlikely of early adoption. We are still in the position that Jefferson encountered. Writing of his plan in 1814, he said: "My hopes, however, are kept in check by . . . our state legislature." [2]

The objectives toward which we should look as immediately practicable include the nationwide prohibition of the gainful employment of children below sixteen years of age; the improvement of school facilities for all ages, the better adaptation of school curricula to the needs and capacities of different groups—differentiated according to mental ability and aptitudes, and only secondarily and temporarily to economic status; the establishment of full opportunity for adult education.

[2] Mayo, *Jefferson Himself*, Houghton, Mifflin, 1942, p. 324.

Such a program can hardly become possible without a federal subsidy to the states of low per capita income. If and when such subsidies are made possible they should be made available only to states which grant equal privileges to all of their citizens.

A consideration of what we have to do in the field of civil rights brings us face to face with the problem of race relations. While such rights may be and sometimes are denied to others it is the Negro race that has suffered most. To recount instances of discrimination would be time-consuming and wholly unnecessary, for they are legion and widely known. They involve interference with the rights of citizens in economic, political, social and human relations. No greater condemnation of our claims to be a democratic people can be pronounced than that which we have written for ourselves in our record of relations with the Negro race.

This is a social problem of first magnitude, but it is also a labor problem both because one of the most active and ever present forms of discrimination is in the field of employment and because hostility is not limited to the employer but is manifest also on the part of white labor, even including a considerable part of the labor movement itself.

If the postwar world is to be one in which we live up to our pretensions, we shall have much housecleaning to do in this field. As a matter of fact we cannot wait for the end of the war. As others have said in better words than mine, we shall not be able to convince the world and particularly the Asiatic world that we are genuinely fighting for democracy unless we give evidence now of a determination to end a reign of injustice based on false claims of racial superiority.

I do not underestimate the difficulties involved in dealing with this problem. There is no simple or easy solution. I doubt if we can accomplish it by restrictive laws and punitive action. We must restrain those who would violate the law, but we must at the same time seek to discover and remove the underlying causes. I suspect that ignorance and economic insecurity lie at the root of the matter, and that we must solve these two problems before we can hope for a general and effective response to the ethical appeal for justice.

That is why I think it is basic in any social program for postwar reconstruction that we liberate all men, white and black, from the hampering chains of destitution and ignorance.

The forces upon which we must depend for bringing about the changes previously discussed are two: action by organized society through the state, and action by citizens, organized in voluntary groups. The most important of the latter, for purposes of the present discussion, is organized labor.

In any acceptable forecast of our society in the time to come, organized labor must be taken for granted as a growing and essential force. There are now eleven or twelve million members of unions in the United States. Impressively large as this number is, it is only about a third of the wage-earning population. The continued growth of organized labor in the postwar period is to be expected and encouraged.

The relation of organization to the economic interests of the workers is obvious. When organized labor speaks in the conference room through its representatives it possesses a bargaining strength that is wholly lacking to the individual who attempts to negotiate a wage contract by himself. A man of unique abilities—a Caruso, a Babe Ruth, a Barrymore—may be able to bargain more successfully for himself than he could through an organization of fellow craftsmen but it is not so for the rank and file. Few of them are indispensable; most of them are easily replaced. But when they stand together as a group these weaknesses disappear.

Moreover, both the size of modern industry and its corporate form make collective bargaining essential. "No man," a corporation executive said to me many years ago, "is wise enough to know what is good for a thousand other men, without the advice of these men."

Organization is important to the workers also because it enables them to function as an interest group in community, state, and nation. Government is of necessity, and with increasing intensity, concerning itself both with the welfare of the wage earner and with relationships between employee and employer. In the choice of public officials, in the making of laws and in the decisions of administrative bodies, labor is coming to have a greater and greater stake. In their relation to these things, the unorganized workers are as weak and inarticulate as the individual bargainer facing the corporation executive. No one can speak for a million separate individuals. But the spokesmen for twelve million organized workers have the willing ear of lawmakers and presidents.

Beyond these considerations there is something else that is, possibly, of still greater significance. Belonging to a union becomes important to the individual because it contributes to his sense of personal worth and dignity. Golden and Ruttenberg tell of the formation of a union among employees of a firm that had previously paid good wages and catered in many ways to the welfare of the employees. In spite of this the workers were insistent in their demand for a union and collective bargaining. They were

> concerned with getting things out that had been bottled up inside of them for all these years, and with contemplating the prospect of being able to do things for themselves that would give a meaning to their personalities and a purpose to their lives. The paternalistic policies of management—doing the thinking for its employees, giving them things, and trying zealously to keep everybody happy—made these workers feel subservient when they wanted to be proud, and made them seek that something that was terribly important to them but lacking in their rigid industrial life.

It is a prime necessity therefore that in the postwar era all of the devices that we have set up to protect the worker's right to organization and collective bargaining—the anti-injunction laws, the labor relations acts—should be retained and strengthened. The full maintenance of the democratic basis of our society depends upon it.

But we may not leave this subject without recognizing and facing certain weaknesses and dangers in the labor movement. I have already mentioned the fact that certain unions maintain an official policy of hostility toward members of the Negro race. Many of them will not admit Negroes to membership, however competent they may be. Others, having admitted them, relegate them to an inferior position within the union, giving them a second-rate membership with lesser voting privileges than the white members possess, or no voice at all in major union policies.

It is refreshing to note some outstanding illustrations of the opposite of this policy. The C.I.O. Automobile Workers Union, for example, dealt last fall with a strike of white workers in a single plant against the employment of Negroes in that plant, by offering the strikers the alternative of returning to work or loss of union membership. The strikers yielded. Many unions do admit Negroes to membership on a basis of full equality. But the contrary policy of other unions is fixed and adamant.

In many unions there is a disturbing lack of democratic procedure. High officers in some cases keep themselves in control by postponing the calling of conventions or in other ways preventing the holding of elections, in violation of their own constitutions. In some unions the officers have accomplished the same ends by securing the adoption of undemocratic amendments to their union constitutions, providing for indefinite tenure. To a certain extent, even in the unions honestly and intelligently led, there is a tendency toward centralization of authority that seems to go beyond what is required for efficient management, and to threaten democratic control.

Another tendency that might be mentioned is the paying of extravagant salaries to union officials. This, I think, is understandable as an extension of a disease that has fastened itself upon the business community. It is supposed that men will not give loyal service unless they are offered an "incentive" that has all the earmarks of a bribe. This had led to the payment of hundred thousand dollar salaries to presidents of bankrupt railroads and in the industrial world to the device of a bonus which, added to salary, has sometimes provided executives with fantastic annual incomes, even reaching the quarter million mark, or more. Labor officials are not in this class. The highest salary of a union executive that I know about is twenty-five thousand dollars. But this seems to me too high for anyone to accept from the dues of workers who have not yet achieved for themselves the essentials of economic security.

I do not emphasize racketeering and crime among the unions for two reasons: First, such activities are not characteristic of unionism generally. The majority of unions do their work without claiming the attention either of the district attorney or the writer of newspaper headlines. Moreover, the membership of unions is made up in the enormous majority of honest men and women—a fair cross section of the society in which they live.

The second reason grows out of the first: since the unions are made up of representative members of society, it is not surprising that there should be some among them who are willing to disregard the rules. Neither business, nor the professions, nor the church is without its proportion of lawbreakers. It is not without significance that last spring on the day that a notorious union racketeer made his richly merited entrance into Sing Sing Prison he might have met the former president of the New York Stock Exchange coming out.

I do, however, take issue with the idea that the honest leaders of organized labor cannot take active measures to rid the union movement of its crooks and criminals because of the alleged "autonomy" of the particular units involved. They are not without means of disciplining recalcitrant members and they make use of these means in issues of lesser importance to society.

If in the postwar world we continue to protect the unions in their right to exist and to function, as I think we should, we have a right to ask them to do something about some of the practices that are the subject of public criticism. If they fail, and union policy is not made to accord with public policy, these matters do not lie outside the realm of justifiable public control. Possibly unions should be required by law to hold elections at regular intervals and by secret ballot, such elections to be supervised by public officials, just as the elections to choose agencies for representation are now supervised by the National Labor Relations Board. The undemocratic practice of excluding Negro workers from full and equal membership in unions might be dealt with by withdrawing from such unions the protection of the National Labor Relations Act.

Crime in itself, and at the moment of occurrence, is a matter solely for the law-enforcing authorities. Public action should be in the direction of strengthening these authorities and stimulating them to action. It would seem reasonable, however, to bar from the further holding of office in any union any person who in the exercise of his functions as union official has violated the penal laws.

So far, perhaps, the state should go in the regulation of union affairs. It is unlikely that it should go further, since self-regulation is far more effective than compulsion. At any rate, the burden of proof that further regulation is desirable rests very positively on those who advocate it. The offering of such proof may turn out to be a little difficult for those who at the same time are asking for a relaxation of government control over business, in the name of a theory of free enterprise. Furthermore, no proposal for curbing union activity should be made without thoughtful consideration of the economic and legal handicaps now characteristic of the status of the wage earner. As long as these handicaps are allowed to remain, there can be little equity in proposals to subject unions to very much of public regulation.

Postwar labor problems in America will depend for their solution on the degree of intelligence, toleration and good will with which they are approached. The material prerequisites to establishing a sound economic order, based on justice and fair distribution of products, are in our hands. We have proved that we can utilize our productive capacity to the utmost in the manufacture of the munitions of war and thereby practically abolish unemployment. We shall emerge from the war immensely better equipped with tools, plants and technological knowledge than we were when the war began. Our natural resources will continue to be adequate to our needs. We shall have both the tools and the human capacity to produce the necessities and the comforts of life more quickly, more cheaply and in greater abundance than ever before.

We are now using these vast resources to produce agencies of destruction, and we are doing that in order to preserve forever our right to use them for human advancement. It is inconceivable that when we have accomplished that purpose we shall fail to utilize the very thing for which we fought.

We can abolish unemployment and want. We can assure economic security to an entire nation. We can do these things if, as Sir William Beveridge says, we care enough to "take the trouble."

THE EMERGING ROLE OF GOVERNMENT

By

EDMUND De S. BRUNNER, Ph.D.

Professor of Education, Teachers College, Columbia University

The assigned title of this paper describes a social phenomenon of vast importance. If one listens to the conversations in Pullman cars, one may imagine that this trend started on March 4, 1933. This is, to put it mildly, not an accurate description of the situation. It may be worthwhile to take a hasty backward glance over the past two centuries. In 1743 and before, the agrarian-craft society of Europe was operating under a socio-economic organization that had been worked out in terms of the necessities of life. In contrast with the sixteenth century it reflected the readjustments made necessary by the far ranging discoveries of Europe's mariners and the movement of population to the newly opened areas. The horizons, physical and mental, of the European world were widening. The old controls were proving increasingly hampering to the fulfillment of desires stimulated by new opportunities. Three revolutions were brewing.

The first of these was political. Our fathers brought forth on this continent a new nation dedicated to liberty. Nothing else could have come out of North America where northern Europeans faced a whole new continent which was theirs to exploit and make serve the purposes of men who had permanently parted from the restrictive physical and social arrangements of the old world.

The second revolution was industrial. A British workman, taking a day off, got curious about the power that lifted the lid of a tea kettle. That curiosity changed the aspect of the world. The industrial-power age was born and of its own offspring there is as yet no end.

The third revolution was ideological. True, ideas had played their part in the political changes in America and France. But it remained for Adam Smith to give the rationalization for the lifting of the old controls of agrarian-craft society. With a vision of plenty, of untold wealth seemingly within grasp, liberty in economic life seemed the necessary concomitant of political freedom. And the gospel of Adam Smith, as amended by John Stuart Mill, still has myriads of devotees and many minor prophets such as Herbert Hoover.

But there is one qualification Smith and Mill both made which today is often forgotten by their successors. Both indicated that if men selfishly abused the privileges of liberty, if they interfered with the automatic workings of the principle of *laissez faire,* government would have to step in to control such selfishness. Any theologian trained in the Judaic-Christian teaching as to the nature of man could have told Adam Smith what to expect at this point. And it happened. Hence Mill went so far as to argue that there could properly be protection of the consumer, compulsory public education, regulation and control of stock companies, charity and welfare activities and so on, without damage to the essential operation of society. And almost half a century before Mill, our government began to play with protective tariffs, certainly an interference with the free operation of economic forces.

This is an all too hasty summary of a vitally important and exciting social process but the years between then and now must be all but omitted for our purposes and under our time limitations. Suffice it to say that our governmental framework was set up under the influence of the first and third of these revolutions. Liberty and the pursuit of happiness were perforce to be achieved under the influence of the socio-economic experiences men had had prior to the industrial revolution. Our fathers were too preoccupied with the struggle for political independence in 1776 even to know about Watts and his tea kettle, let alone envisage the implications for the infant nation we then were.

Hence as new functions were added to government over the decades because of the impact of social and economic forces, they ran ahead of the structure of government. Thus the Public Health Service of the United States was until recently attached to the Treasury

Department. Public health began with medical examinations of passengers and crews at ports of entry. Hence health officers had to work side by side with customs inspectors. What more natural than to give this function to the Treasury? The outstanding current illustration of this tendency is the Federal Security Agency, important also because it shows the process by which the dilemma caused by the lag between function and structure is being worked out. In this agency we now at long last have a consolidation of most of the various services dealing with welfare. Some were born in the depression. Others came from the Departments of Interior, Labor, the Treasury. Yet this new organization is an agency, not an executive department, despite the fact that its budget and personnel are larger than those of several departments. It is not yet wholly within the accepted structural framework of our federal government. Its head therefore does not sit in the cabinet and, for instance, manpower problems must be settled not in the cabinet but by a committee made up of cabinet members and the joint head of the Federal Security Agency and the Manpower Commission.

As several needs and problems tend to force government to take on new functions these new agencies are set up. The meeting of the need, the function to be performed, is institutionalized. These new agencies then proceed according to the laws of institutions, laws traced from observation of behavior by our sociologists. One of these laws is that social institutions tend to try to perpetuate themselves. It follows that any successful growth of a new agency, especially by the accretion of new functions may not be approved by all of the citizens, though it is seldom that a new agency is ended as in recent months the CCC and WPA have been. But these were emergency organizations. They ended as did the National Council of Defense after World War I when the emergency that created it had passed, though like it they made the inevitable effort to achieve institutional immortality.

The years from 1870 to 1930 furnish a number of illustrations of the assumption by government of new functions. Increased services were made available to commerce, industry and agriculture and there soon followed policing or control functions. The Interstate

Commerce Commission and the founding of the agricultural experiment stations are two among many illustrations. Public works, especially flood control and highways, began to expand. The Public Health Service was a protective and soon a welfare agency for the benefit of all. Natural resources engaged governmental attention, involving everything from the construction, development and operation of national parks to the far-flung activities of research. Private capital saw no profitable return from railroad building in Alaska or operating a steamship line to the swamps of Panama, and so two profitable businesses have been paying dividends to Uncle Sam with no anguished charges of socialism to disturb their operation. Excursions were made into the realm of education in the subsidizing of vocational education in the schools, and in agriculture and home economics extension work for the farm population. As a result of these trends non-military federal expenses by the middle of Mr. Hoover's term had risen over 200% from 1915, though measured in terms of the purchasing power of money the increase was a trifle under 100%.

With the intensification of the depression which coincided with the first administration of our present chief executive, government assumed many new roles. Before discussing some of these and their implications, however, it is necessary to examine the fundamental situation which the nation faced in the winter of 1932–33.

Even in 1929 at the end of a decade so prosperous that those high in authority dared to envisage perpetual prosperity, the conservative Brookings Institution's studies showed among other things:

1. That over 42% of our families had incomes of less than $1500, 71% less than $2500. The income of the 42% of the families with less than $1500 roughly equaled that of the 1/10 of 1% of the families with incomes of $75,000 and over. There was clearly a great concentration of income and wealth in relatively few hands.

2. That even in 1929, and making every possible allowance, our productive machine was turning out only 4/5 of the goods it was capable of producing. Had it been able to reach this practical, engineering 100% (as contrasted with theoretic maximum capacity) the ad-

ditional wealth produced if so distributed could have brought all those with incomes of $2000 or less up to that level.

Came the depression. National income dropped to less than half the 1929 level. The wealthy were hard hit but the ⅖ of the population at the bottom of the income scale, lacking the cushion of savings, rapidly fell in large numbers to the destitution level. Groups here and there, like the farmers in the 1870's and 1920's, had suffered severely before but this depression, our worst, revealed as never before how close to danger a large proportion of our population really were. The industrial and economic mechanisms of the country struggled to stem the avalanche. Their failure was dramatized for us by the bank holiday of March, 1933. There appeared only one agency that could avert a complete national debacle—namely government, which in this country is we, the people, society as a whole, acting through representatives and their authorized employees.

It is not within my province or purpose today to diagnose the causes responsible for this situation. Much ink has been devoted to that theme. I do, however, wish to point to a part of one diagnosis because it bears on my assigned theme. In the latter half of the 1930's *Fortune* published a remarkable series of editorials on Government and Business. It pointed out a number of the mistakes of business that had contributed to our slow recovery, such things as administered prices which remained unadjusted to our halved income and which were made possible by our huge concentrations of capital and therefore of power. It pointed out that such interferences in practice with the philosophy business still expressed, compelled society to intervene. Government had become big and powerful because business had become big and powerful and because of the way that bigness and that power had been used. Adam Smith never foresaw the developments of the twentieth century. His book was published the same year Watts got interested in turning tea kettles into engines. But there are passages in Smith and Mill that imply clearly the thing which the editors of *Fortune* say has come to pass.

What, then, are some of the things government has done? What new roles has it assumed?

For one thing it has assumed far beyond anything in the past history of our land a welfare function. If there is one word that future historians may use more than any other to characterize the first two Roosevelt administrations it will perhaps be the word Security.

There was no great use for that word in the nineteenth century. The man with restricted opportunity, yes, even the failure, could solve his problems by deserting them and joining the westward trek. There was undeveloped land. There were natural resources to be discovered and exploited. There the individual could build his own security with his own head and hands. But by 1933, and before, that was no longer possible and no new invention like the automobile appeared to employ idle hands that itched for work.

The Social Security Board set up a great scheme of unemployment insurance and old age pensions. The Federal Security Agency among other things expanded the work in public health, child care, pensions for widowed mothers. The WPA and its predecessors gave socially useful employment at minimum wages to millions of persons. The NYA and the CCC tried to help youth for whom society could find no place or who were threatened with a loss of the privilege of education which our society values very highly. The Farm Security Administration sought to alleviate the plight of tractored-out or burned-out farmers from the Dust Bowl and the Southwest, and of the sharecroppers and others in the older sections.

The efficiency of these agencies varied. Details and in some cases major aspects of their programs are far from being above criticism. That is not the point in terms of our present discussion. The point is that society was faced with an unprecedented emergency. From fourteen to fifteen million at one time were without the means of providing for themselves and their dependents the primary necessities of food, clothing and shelter. The accustomed mechanisms of society for fulfilling such needs had broken down. Society as a whole, government, was used to make these fundamental necessities for biological survival available.

Except for local governmental units' care of their few indigent and the states' care of such unfortunates as the mentally ill and the tubercular, this was a new role for our government. But it should be pointed out that in other governments, including democracies, it was not new. The United States was a late recruit to such policies. The trend began in Germany under Bismarck, in England, Australia and New Zealand around the turn of the century. It was present in Scandinavia. It was new only to us, in terms only of our experience.

Were there time it would be interesting to trace the development of this idea from relief to security, from charity to a concept that reasonable security is the right of a citizen in a democracy. Speaking under these auspices it is certainly fitting to point out that the social obligation to care for the fatherless and the widow, for the destitute and the oppressed, is inherent in the religious traditions in which all of us have been reared. From the date of Leviticus on, it has been made clear that this was what God required. Indeed even in the 1930's there were religious groups living in what might be called cultural islands, or closed cultural systems, able to care for their own successfully. The question whether religion has lost a function in whole or part or whether the teachings of religion and the examples of churches convinced society that it must act as it did when the crisis came, is interesting but outside our province today.

Will government surrender this role which has emerged so clearly in the United States during this past decade? I doubt it extremely. We have currently, with the business index running about double the 1935–39 level, a demonstration such as few deemed possible, of the power of America to produce goods. The ordinary run of citizens will be unimpressed with the subtleties of the credit mechanism, or the price-wage-credit relationships if told that they interfere with the attainment of security. They will demand that what we have demonstrated in war we continue in peace, and above all that demand will come from men who are risking their lives to maintain the American way of life and from those who are engaged in the production of war goods which we all hope will soon be largely unnecessary in a world that has regained some measure of sanity. Unless the more familiar or older devices succeed fully, with the help of some of the new mechanisms such as unemployment insurance in solving postwar economic problems on the home front, government will be called upon to continue in the role it has assumed with respect to security since 1933. Moreover, I suspect that this will be tied to a public works policy of real scope. Probably no private corporation could have built the Grand Coulee dam with all that it means in the development of power and the increase of food producing acreage. But who doubts the economic and social profit of that enterprise in terms of balance sheets prepared not on an annual basis but by decades or quarter centuries?

There are two other elements in the emerging role of government of which I wish to speak in the time remaining. Policy making or planning has been carried far beyond the regulatory provisions of the past such as the Federal Trade Commission, the enforcement of the Sherman Act or even the Securities Exchange Commission of more recent vintage. One example of that is the TVA. It has produced a peaceful and desirable revolution in a basic region of the United States. Its dividends are measurable in social and educational terms as well as in the more familiar indices of economics. But I wish to take another illustration—the Agricultural Adjustment Acts. Here for the first time the United States constructed a national agricultural policy geared to the realities of the domestic and international scenes. There were a number of unique features in that legislation. The Act of 1933 provided, as had no other law, for a high degree of flexibility. When the objective of parity prices for any crop had been attained the Secretary of Agriculture was empowered to end the benefit payments. In other words the farmers were ready to accept a ceiling on their profits from the Act.[1] The determination of the point at which action should be taken was left to the economists of the Department of Agriculture. This was a recognition, first, of the danger to society of waiting for politico-legal action by Congress to adjust operations to rapidly changing social conditions, and secondly, of the great advances in social science that made it possible to base such decisions upon research. Again the law was and is flexible in that it provides, within the framework of the adequate conservation of our basic resource—the soil; for the expan-

[1] It is in my judgment most unfortunate that this provision was eliminated from the second AAA, as a result of the invalidation of the first Act by the Supreme Court.

sion of production as well as for the restriction of production in some crops and the shift of such freed acreage to other and more desirable products.

Another unusual feature of the first act as well as of the present one was the provision that the program for any crop in any given year was to become effective only when approved by the growers of that crop. In cases where it seemed necessary to apply restrictive quotas to production the law requires a two-thirds majority before it becomes operative. It is significant that the majorities with reference to the various crops in these annual elections over the last decade have ranged from just under 90% of all votes cast up to over 98%. Moreover the checking of compliance with the several programs agreed upon in these elections has been in the hands not of a new police force nor regulatory bureaucracy but of committees of farmers elected by their peers in every agricultural township and county in the land.

Here surely is something new in the application of our theory of government. The elected representatives of the people in the usual manner have passed a law which sets up policies in principle affecting every farm in the nation. But the operation of those policies is not dictated. It is based year after year on plans developed by social scientists, submitted to the test of the approval of those most concerned, and on the level of local operation is administered by those concerned. Australia has adopted a similar device in some of her legislation.

To me this is extremely significant despite the admitted imperfections of the Act. In these days when—leaving war out of account —government is being invested with more and more power by what we recognize as democratic procedures on the national level, we have constructed a social mechanism that within broad limits puts the decision in the hands of those concerned and that permits the individual to conform or not to that decision as he sees fit unless quotas have been voted, or in other words unless his fellow producers decide that an emergency exists.

Perhaps here is a device, properly adapted to varying situations, which will enable us to take advantage of the power of government in these new areas into which it is advancing, and at the same time not merely preserve our essential democracy but rather bring its operation down to the level and within the decision of the ordinary citizen.

Frankly, I am at a loss for a single term like security or policy making to describe the last point I wish to make. There are some who would argue that what I am about to discuss is nothing but an extension of the regulatory function or the umpire function long exercised by government. There are others who would say it is an illustration of the way the power of government can be prostituted to the advantage of specific groups. Technically I suppose the first description is the more accurate, though heaven and earth both know that government can be manipulated for the selfish purposes of particular interests. I refer to the type of legislation and of government functioning illustrated by exempting cooperatives from the operation of the Sherman anti-trust law, and to the National Labor Relations Act.

Anyone who, like your speaker, worked along with others in the latter half of this century's first decade for eleven and twelve hours a day for from $3 to $10 a week, knows that labor can be exploited. Anyone who studies the occupational distribution of the labor force of this country and also the occupational choices of high-school youth, knows that the old ambition to achieve a white collar job because of the idea that such work meant success is an unrealistic day dream, despite the proportionate increases in the professional and other service occupations which seem destined to continue.

But anyone who knows the people of these United States knows that the American dream of achieving freedom, happiness and the abundant life is as vivid in the consciousness of our citizens as it ever was. Essentially what the organization of farmers and labor means to me is this: that we the people have realized that it is foolish for every American boy to try to get as close to being President as possible; that rather the American dream can be realized in terms of standard of living, that technology has made short hours, education, automobiles and gadgets, nutritive food, leisure and hence recreation, safely possible without destroying the incentives of capital;

that indeed the desire for such an adequate standard of living is but an extension to all in terms fitting each group of the very incentives that motivate the possessors and managers of capital; that since farmers and workers are separate individuals, organization is necessary to secure the equivalent of what a corporation possesses; that such organization in our present structure is an inherent right under our democracy, an application of the principles of the founding fathers to these areas; that since the effort to achieve this interpretation of the American dream means a larger share of the power and profits of our society for some than they formerly had and since there is as yet no formula for determining such distribution, so that conflict arises, government must assume the role of facilitating the achievement of these purposes.

After all, farmers and laborers are citizens, they are part of "we the people." They may propose measures that would only harm them as in my judgment some farm groups now are doing. But the necessary limitations upon unrestricted operations of capital, just as the necessary limitations upon national interest if we are to achieve an ordered world, are discussable in practical terms because science has made them safely possible. The 1930's surely made tragically self-evident the truth that only by sustaining the standard of living of all can society function safely and profitably.

The laws alluded to in this connection and others prove that at the moment we have made up our minds that government is to be used to help all who fail to achieve a standard of living and of life commensurate with the ideals and purposes of our society. Moreover the basic values implicit in this conception are derived from religion with its high regard for the individual and his personality.

I have been dealing throughout and especially in these last moments with matters of violent controversy. Inevitably we have made mistakes, some serious, and we will make more. But what we see in the at first slow and then more rapid assumption by government of new functions and roles is an adaptation to new conditions and new problems growing out of new knowledge and its application to the affairs of men. Certainly there has been an essential consistency in aim as this evolution has unfolded.

In a democracy government and the people are one and inseparable. Government is but a mechanism devised by the people to facilitate their collective life. Examine the policies of a democratic government and you can read the slow unfolding of national purposes as they grow and crystallize out of the bitter competition of ideas in the market place of public opinion. There can be no permanent drawing back from our attempt to make life safer both from the hazards of living and from the results of our mistakes in managing our economy. There can be no drawing back from the effort to achieve a good life for Americans all. In these efforts we are utilizing government. Our job is to achieve what we are struggling for by putting more and more content and power into the functioning of our democratic ideals. That has been our pathway, our way of life, for nearly two centuries. That way was never more threatened than at present. By the same token it has never seemed more precious.

OPINION MAKING IN THE POSTWAR WORLD

By

CLYDE R. MILLER, Ed.D.

Associate Professor of Education,
Teachers College, Columbia University

Opinion making in the postwar world will not differ psychologically from opinion making in the midst of war. It will not differ from opinion making in the past. That is to say, in the postwar world propaganda or persuasion will employ the same methods employed now, the same methods which have always been employed. Inasmuch as it seems mathematically certain that the United Nations will win a military victory and inasmuch as numerous demagogues and even more numerous sincere people will utilize propaganda to prevent the peace from being a democratic peace, it is important to those who hope for a democratic peace to know the methods employed by propagandists.

The most commonly used methods or devices are the following:

I. Name Calling, or the use of "poison" words to bring about disapproval and rejection of a nation, a race, a religion, a program, a plan, an economic or political system.

II. Glittering Generalities, or the use of "Rosy Glow" words. Here the purpose of the propagandist is to obtain approval of a nation, a race, etc.

III. Testimonial, which involves the use of testimony intended to cause disapproval or approval.

IV. Transfer, which is about the same as Testimonial and often is indistinguishable from it. Here the propagandist employs a symbol such as the cross of the church, or the flag, or the cartoonist's figure of Uncle Sam to obtain disapproval or approval.

V. Plain Folks, which reveals the propagandist as plain folks, just like the rest of us, seeking the same goals and believing in the same principles we all believe in—in short, a device to win mass support.

VI. Card Stacking, which the propagandist employs to deceive, or to use sheer falsehoods to obtain approval or disapproval of a nation, a race, etc., he wants approved or disapproved.

VII. Band Wagon, the purpose of which is to indicate that "everybody's doing it" and that, therefore, we ought to get on the band wagon and do it, too—that is, disapprove or approve a nation, a race, etc.

All of these devices in so far as they make quick appeal and get quick response employ the "conditioned reflex." We all know the story of the psychologist, Pavlov, and his animals. Pavlov discovered that the sight of food will cause a dog, say, to salivate. If a bell is rung when food is placed before a dog and if this operation is repeated say sixty or seventy times, it is found that the sound of the bell alone, without food being present, will cause salivation.

The story of a runaway horse in the town of Owego illustrates this:

Not so long ago the Associated Press carried a short story out of Owego, New York. It was about a runaway horse. It seems this horse was hitched to a milk wagon. While the driver was delivering milk to a restaurant on the main street of Owego, the horse started down the street lickity-cut—a runaway!

The Chief of Police, the story went on, was on a motorcycle two or three blocks to the rear. He saw the runaway start. He turned on the gas and soon caught up with the horse. Just as he did so, the horse reached the main traffic intersection of Owego. At that moment, the traffic light turned red. The horse stopped so quickly that he slid on his haunches.

The Chief of Police was quoted in the final sentence of the AP story as saying, "I got him by the bridle before the light turned green."

It is obvious that this runaway horse was conditioned to stop on red and go on green, just as human beings driving automobiles are conditioned to do the same. When people as well as animals are conditioned to react automatically to some stimulus, whether it be a bell, a light, a word, a phrase or a symbol, it is as though part of the brain had drained down into the spinal cord.

An enormous amount of our actions really are reactions. A word is spoken, or a symbol is displayed and thanks to our conditioning, thanks to our brains being in our spinal cords, we are likely to react exactly the way the propagandist wants us to react. These reactions are seen most clearly, perhaps, in the common Name Calling and Glittering Generalities devices. Again, let me illustrate:

Seated in the living room of my brother's home in Detroit, Michigan, on a very hot summer day two or three years ago, I was talking to my brother's wife when a big black dog walked into the room.

"That's Dixie," said my brother's wife. "He is a smart dog. Let me show you."

And then she said, "Dixie, shut the door."

The dog walked over to the front door, put a big black paw against it and pushed it shut.

"See," she said, "isn't he a smart dog?" I allowed he was. Then I reconsidered and said, "But maybe he isn't smart after all. The only breath of air we are getting in this room was coming in from the front porch and Dixie has shut that off. If this dog really were smart, he would turn on the electric fan."

It was obvious that the phrase "shut the door" was the stimulus which caused Dixie to react and actually push the door shut.

Another illustration:

I have a friend, Fred C. Kelly, the writer. He asked me to dinner a few years ago, shortly before the war, at his fine home near the little village of Peninsula, Ohio.

Just the two of us were there for the dinner, Fred and I. While we waited for the cook to announce the meal, we sat on the sofa in the living room. On the floor were about six large dogs. Presently the cook announced that dinner was ready. Fred said to the dogs, "Go on, boys, get out." He went to the front door, and the dogs immediately filed out—except one rather biggish dog which apparently was reluctant to go.

"Shep," said Fred, "you don't want to go out, do you? Well, I'll tell you what you may do. You go into the dining room and lie down on the rug. And don't you budge from the spot after you lie down. We have a guest with us tonight and I don't want you to bother him." The dog went into the dining room and lay down.

We followed and took our places at the table. After the soup course, the cook brought in a platter on which was a magnificent steak. The aroma filled the room.

As Fred cut the steak, I felt a slight tug at my left trouser cuff. I knew it was Shep. I knew he had inched over and had hidden himself under the table. He was now saying to me in his own way, "Mister, that smells so good. Won't you *please* give me some of it!"

I didn't want to give Shep away because Fred had cautioned him not to disturb me. However, when the cook, a Chinese gentleman, handed me my plate with a nice piece of steak on it, he interposed himself for just a moment between Fred and me. In that moment, I took a quick look down.

I looked into a pair of pleading brown eyes, brimming with tears. "Won't you *please,* Mister!" Shep pleaded. I quickly looked up as I cut into my meat. Something happened. A stern look immediately came over Fred's face. He pushed back his chair, stood up and said, "Shep, the idea, disturbing Mr. Miller that way. Get right out of here!"

The dog made an end run around by the fireplace, through the double doors and into the living room. Fred after him.

The dog went back into the dining room and lay down. Fred resumed his place at the table. I found out that Fred had not seen Shep but that the dog, in his eagerness for the meat had violently wagged his tail and that just the end of the wagging tail had come within Fred's vision.

Well, it wasn't long before the temptation again was too great for Shep. This time I felt a heavy paw on my lap and looked down involuntarily. "Shep," said Fred, "what do you mean by annoying a guest that way. Now you get!"

The dog ran to the outer door, Fred after him. This time Fred had his hand on the door knob. To my surprise Fred said, "Shep, it just occurs to me you missed your feeding today when the other dogs were fed. I know you are very hungry and I am going to give you one final chance. You must learn to obey. I am going to give you a piece of meat, however, to stay your stomach."

Fred went to the table, took a piece of meat from the platter and threw it across the room to the hearth of the fireplace.

From where I sat I could see Shep's throat muscles get tense. He was on the meat at a bound. I knew as soon as his teeth touched it it would go down in one gulp. Well, he got it in his mouth and the act of swallowing was just beginning when Fred Kelly yelled out one word:

"Poison."

The dog stood there trembling as though the meat were a living coal of fire. I said, "Fred, get him out of it and tell me how you did it!"

Fred said, "Shep, as I give this matter more mature deliberation, as I take into account various factors in this situation, I come to the conclusion that this piece of meat is eatable. If you want to eat it I would say it is perfectly all right." When Fred pronounced the words "perfectly all right" his pronunciation of them was beneficently soothing—the dog ate the meat.

"How did you do it?" I asked.

"Well," replied Fred, "it is nothing more than Pavlov's conditioned reflex. I brought this dog up from puppyhood. I gave him his first solid food. I would place a piece of meat in his mouth, and when he started to swallow it I would take it from him and at the same time rap him smartly over the muzzle with a pencil or my finger and say 'poison.' After I had done this about sixty-five times it was unnecessary for me to take the meat or whatever the thing might be from Shep's mouth or to rap him on the muzzle. All I needed to do was to say the word 'poison.' If Shep were within earshot, he would drop what was in his mouth."

"But, Fred," I said, "how do you get him to eat the meat?"

"By using the conditioned reflex," said Fred, "but with this difference: the stimulus to get him to eat the meat is not a single word like 'poison' but rather the soothing inflection I give the final word or phrase when I suggest that the meat is all right.

"I do not have to use the word 'all right.' For example, recently

I had a chemist here, an old friend of mine. Then, as now, I made Shep drop the meat by calling it 'poison.' When I wanted him to eat it I gave quite a talk on food chemistry, ending up with the sentence: 'Shep, I think this meat is eatable. I would say it is chemically pure.' I pronounced the words 'chemically pure' just as I pronounced the word 'all right' tonight. To get this reaction, the stimulus is done by voice rather than the word itself."

Fred Kelly's dog illustrates perfectly the propaganda device of Name Calling and Rosy Glow.

Propagandists have always used Name Calling to get an immediate automatic response of disapproval and rejection. The very word "poison" is a stimulus which will cause any of us to reject a food or anything else that we think may injure us. If the word is correctly used, our automatic response to the stimulus is all to the good; it may save our life. If the word is incorrectly used, our automatic response to it may keep us from enjoying something which is not poison at all. A century ago, for example, tomatoes were widely regarded as poison. They were grown in front yards as ornamental shrubs, to be seen and admired but not to be eaten. It required analysis, investigation, experimentation to prove that they were not poison but that they were very good for us. It is easy to think of any number of examples similar to this.

In the Middle Ages the word heretic was used as a poison word. Any person who was called a heretic was likely to be put to death by torture. To both Protestants and Catholics heretic was a poison word. It required analysis and the scientific method to reveal that many who were labeled heretic were not evil persons at all.

Take the word "Jew." For more than eighteen hundred years the people of Christendom had been conditioned to react automatically and unfavorably to that word. It was poison. In Europe during the Middle Ages Jews were an out-group. Their religion was regarded as inferior to the Christian religion, they were regarded as inferior to Christians. They lived in ghettos and were subject to restrictions and persecutions, much the same way as Negroes in America live in segregated areas and must endure Jim Crow restrictions.

The sanction of the Christian church approved the segregation of

Jews and their status of inferiority. Thus the Transfer device operated through the church to transfer the authority of God himself to the onus placed upon Jews.

In our own times we have seen how President Roosevelt used the poison words "Tory" and "economic royalist" as stimuli to bring about immediate automatic rejection of those who were opposing his election.

The most successful propagandist, however, is Adolf Hitler. He uses the word "Jew" in his propaganda precisely because hundreds of millions of Christians had been conditioned to react negatively and automatically at the sound or sight of the word. By blaming the loss of the First World War and the inflation and the depression on Jews, and offering himself as a leader who would destroy this enemy and thus free Germans and all Christians from the sinister Jewish evil, Hitler was able to evoke precisely the automatic response he wanted. He got a mass following.

By using the poison word "Communism" he obtained the support of eminent industrialists, business men, bankers, churchmen, journalists, and statesmen not only in Germany but in England, France and America. To such men the word "Communism" or one of its equivalents meant social revolution; it meant the overthrow of the economic-political system with which these men and their institutions were identified. Their support of Hitler operated as Testimonial; it functioned as Transfer, conveying to Hitler and his Nazi Party the prestige and sanction and following of eminent figures of the church, of the business world, of journalism and of government.

Within six months after Hitler came to power the Vatican signed a concordat with him. To millions of people this action—whether the Vatican willed it or not—was tantamount to something like approval of Hitler and the Nazi Party on the part of the Vatican—particularly when considered along with the Vatican's continuous denunciation of "atheistic Communism."

When the Vatican backed Franco, Hitler's man in Spain, the impression that it was also friendly to Hitler was strengthened—again the operation of the Transfer device.

Even stronger approval of Hitler was seen in the words used by the head of the Oxford Movement, later known as Moral Rearmament, Dr. Frank Buchman. Returning to America from Germany and England in 1936, he was quoted in the *New York World Telegram* in August of that year as saying "I thank God for Adolf Hitler. He has saved all Europe from the anti-Christ of Communism. . . ." As we review the foreign policy of France and England from 1930 on we see how that policy operated again and again to support Hitler in building up the Nazi government. It was obvious to analysts who knew their politics and propaganda that Hitler was regarded by the highest authorities, and indeed to no little extent in our country, as our greatest safeguard against "Communism."

Hitler's supreme triumph as a propagandist is seen in the fact that he identified Communism and Jews, and democracy and Communism. He knew that democracy meant freedom to analyze, freedom to criticize. He knew that a Fascist system could not endure if analysis and criticism were permitted.

Immediately on coming to power Hitler had stopped all such analysis and criticism. It was not easy to stop it in other nations. Thanks, however, to a small number of demagogues and to a much larger number of sincere people who really feared social revolution, Hitler was able to accomplish a great deal in France, England and America, by associating democracy with Communism and both with Jew. Shortly after becoming head of the Reich he began saying that democracy is the foul and filthy avenue to Jewish Communism.

Thus, by such propaganda, he was able to inspire the establishment of the Christian Front and the rebirth of the Ku Klux Klan in the United States, as well as to give impetus to strong Fascist movements in France and England.

In our own nation we see Hitler's use of Communist as a poison word paralleled in the propaganda of men like Father Coughlin, Westbrook Pegler, Martin Dies, William Randolph Hearst and the Reverend Gerald L. K. Smith.

Here, as in Germany, France and England, the response evoked by the word Communist has been so marked that even as late as February, 1943, Martin Dies could still be cheered by the majority of our House of Representatives and could receive a large vote for the continuation of the Dies Committee, the propaganda pattern of which parallels Hitler's utilization of the poison word Communist. Propagandists utilizing this device count on the brains of most people being in their spinal cords.

As "poison" words make us reject and condemn, so "Rosy Glow" words make us accept. It is said that Hitler has vast admiration for American advertising writers. And well he may!

The purpose of most advertisements is to sell us something. If a cigarette manufacturer can repeat the phrase "Reach for a Lucky" often enough to make us respond automatically and favorably, all he has to do is to keep repeating it so that it continues to operate as a stimulus. Again we see the conditioned reflex. Coca-Cola or Pepsi-Cola are stimuli definitely calculated to make us want a "Coke" whenever we want to quench a thirst refreshingly. Thus, in American advertising, trade names are associated with all manner of Rosy Glow words, phrases and situations.

Note, for example, a full-page advertisement which appeared recently in a magazine. At the top of the page was an attractive line drawing. In the background were patches of woodland; in the middleground, fields of waving grain; in the foreground, an old-fashioned rail fence; in the immediate foreground, an old-fashioned dirt road. Flying above the road about twenty feet in the air was a stork; in his bill, a bundle; in the bundle, a new baby. Coming along the road, doing her best to beat the stork, was an old gray mare, hitched to an old-fashioned buggy, in which sat an old-fashioned doctor, his beard flying in the wind. Obviously it was a race between the doctor and the stork to see who would get there first. Then followed the copy under the caption: Who Was Your First Friend?

Wasn't he the kindly doctor, who ushered you into the world? Then came others . . . parents who taught you love, ethics and honesty . . . youngsters who showed you how to play with teamwork and sportsmanship . . . and teachers who guided you to work with a purpose. As you journey through life, you learn to appreciate the value of friends. Today, when you count your assets, experience tells you that the most priceless of all are your friendships.

Do you know of any better place to sow the seeds of friendship than in the atmosphere of your home? Do you know of any finer symbol of hospitality than Budweiser? Making friends is what made Budweiser the Perfect Host.

Here you see the perfect example of the Rosy Glow device. No wonder Hitler may be said to be indebted to American advertising. The skillful utilization of fair and beautiful words can make people approve and accept not only facial creams, automobiles, modern design cigarettes, and beer—it can also make people approve and accept theories of race, religion, state, empire, economic orders and political systems.

If key words and phrases are associated with fair words charged with a high content of emotion they become stimuli to bring about a conditioned response which automatically approves and accepts; similarly symbols or trade marks become stimuli.

Consider, for example, Adolf Hitler's National Socialist German Workers Party. "National" is a good word in any country. It appeals to our in-group feeling. It suggests that whatever is associated with it is naturally sound and right. Thus in America we call banks national banks. The word gives the impression of soundness and security.

"Socialist" in Germany has as fair a connotation as "welfare" in America. It has for years been associated with old age pensions, improved municipal government, better schools, improved recreation and improved health conditions. To most Germans it was a word just as good as, paradoxically, the word "Communism" is bad.

"German" is to Germans as powerful a stimulus to action which approves and accepts as is the word "American" to Americans.

"Workers" is a favorable word in anybody's country, for the great majority of people are workers.

This word "Party" is the only neutral word in the whole title.

In countless speeches through the '20's and the '30's Hitler and his Nazi associates made the party name a stimulus to approval and acceptance by oratory and ritual (involving Band Wagon and Transfer). Concurrently the Swastika was associated with the party name and all the fair and moving oratory. In this process of conditioning, millions of Germans found in the Swastika symbol itself a stimulus to bring an automatic conditioned response of approval and acceptance.

Similarly, the flag in any nation becomes such a symbol. Likewise, the cross became such a symbol.

Any propagandist, by associating these powerful symbols one with another and by identifying all of them with the program he wants to put across, stands a good chance of succeeding, provided he does not run into too many competing propagandas and provided his propaganda is not directed at people in whom the critical faculty of analysis has been developed.

It is this critical faculty which can make people conscious of their own conditioned reflex, which can cause them to analyze their own response to propagandas and persuasions and to evaluate the goals as well as the methods of the propagandist.

In the postwar world the conditioned reflex will continue to be the strongest ally of propagandists who want immediate automatic response to their stimuli of poison words and rosy-glow phrases. It is certain that following a military victory by the United Nations there will be many propagandists, sincere and insincere, who will use these common devices to swing mass opinion against a peace which might include some surrender of national sovereignty. This happened at the close of World War I. We can see the indications that it will happen at the close of World War II.

As we look at the propaganda of men like Father Coughlin and the Reverend Gerald Winrod we can foresee that the present war will be blamed on the Jews. We can anticipate that here, as in Germany at the close of World War I, the Jews will be regarded, in so far as this propaganda works, as being responsible for the tragedies and suffering of the war.

Despite the fact that "Communism" is losing its power as a poison word for millions who are beginning to have an admiration for the efficiency of the Soviet armies, we may expect it to continue to be so used. We may be sure that a peace consistent with anti-Fascist policy would be labeled "Communist."

One has but to look at Martin Dies and his Congressional committee, one has but to read the Scripps-Howard and the Hearst newspapers to see how Dies and other propagandists such as Hearst and Westbrook Pegler continue to appeal to the fear of social revolution.

Such propagandists, reaching tens of millions through such channels of communication, continue in these days to develop a mental-emotional conditioning that will cause the vast majority of members of the House to extend for a two-year period the Dies Committee.

Out of this same conditioning we discern an automatic favorable response to the propaganda of Captain Eddie Rickenbacker against labor unions.

It may be that Captain Rickenbacker does not know that his propaganda follows the Fascist pattern. Whether he knows it or not, the result is the same. He has become a symbol of heroism—a symbol that tends to evoke automatic acceptance of the Fascist attitude toward labor.

In the continued strength of the propaganda appeals of such men as Dies, Hearst, Westbrook Pegler, Winrod, Coughlin, Rickenbacker and others, there is an indication that the schools, newspapers, churches and other educational and quasi-educational agencies of our country have failed in developing the critical faculty to the extent needed to immunize us against Fascist propaganda.

Such propaganda is our greatest danger—if we believe in the democratic realities and obligations. However much most of us disagree with some of the ideals and obligations of Communism—indeed, the very fact that we do disagree with many of them strengthens this observation—the fact remains that Communism is not any threat to the people of the United States.

A better-planned economy to provide for unemployment and avoid depression, and a better-planned world to provide against future wars, and better-planned teaching of science and religion to provide against racial prejudices—all these things are needed in a democratic peace.

We may be sure that all will be labeled with the poison word "Communist." We may be sure that millions of people will reject any decent and humane peace if it is so labeled—unless, meanwhile and very quickly, the churches and schools of America are able, through an improved type of education, so to develop the critical faculty that millions of us will stop having conditioned reflexes which play into the hands of demagogues. No honest propagandist will object to a type of education which develops the critical faculty. No honest propagandist will object to an analysis of his own propaganda.

What we need and need quickly is an improved type of education to develop the critical faculty, to develop the power of analysis. At the same time it must set up value standards to serve as measuring sticks of human opinions, actions and propagandas.

The very first value standard might well be, "Life ought to be worth living." Most persons will accept this until it is broken down by analysis which asks: "Worth living for whom?" Worth living for just English or Germans or white Americans or Japanese? Should life be worth living for Negroes? Note this news account from the *New York Times* of May 18, 1939, about a man who really believed that life should be worth living for Negroes:

In the May 4 issue of *The Witness,* William B. Spofford, the managing editor, wrote that last summer Bishop Paddock occupied a bed in a hospital ward next to one in which lay a twelve-year-old Negro boy who was dying and knew it. The two patients had long talks and became friends. When the Bishop was able to leave the hospital the boy said to him:

"Let's make an agreement. If I die first, I'll scout out the land on the other side, get the lay-out of the streets, the castles and the palaces. And I'll have a talk with God. I don't believe being a Negro will make any difference with Him. I'll tell Him about you, what a grand guy you are, and I think He'll say: 'O.K., son, when he comes you meet him at the ferry and bring him right to me.' It ought to make it easier. And if you go first, how about putting in a word with God for me?"

The agreement was sealed with a handclasp. A few days later the boy died. During the Bishop's final illness, his nurse told a visitor:

"He's a bit delirious, but he always smiles as he talks, jumbled up words about streets and castles and palaces, and the throne of God, and a colored lad that is soon to meet him at a ferry. Funny the things that pop into the heads of people as they near the end."

Suppose you took that verse from the Scripture which reads, "Suffer the little children to come unto me . . ." and inserted the word Caucasian before the word children—"Suffer the little Caucasian children to come unto me . . ." The whole bottom falls out of the teachings of Jesus.

Our willingness to deny a worthwhile life to Negroes, or Hindus, or Japanese, or Chinese, or Germans, or French seems to be the source of our trouble today. Such denial usually—so far as most people are concerned—is not based upon reason or logic; it is the result of the old conditioned reflex. Jew, or Negro, or East Indian, or Chinese or whatever the group may be is a word which has a stimulus evoking automatic response.

If we are to have a postwar world better than the world we have now we must have a type of education—and very quickly—which will immunize us against indecent and inhumane utilization of our conditioned reflex. Tens of millions of us have got to pull our brains up out of our spinal cords.

There is considerable hope that we will have such a type of education. Indeed it is flourishing already in a good many communities and it has the support of influential church people of all faiths. There are many agencies advocating such a type of education.

One of the best examples, of the many good examples I know of what education can do to make children and adults think with the brains in their heads instead of the fluid in their spinal cords, has been going forward about three years in the public schools of Springfield, Massachusetts.

In Springfield these value standards are set up and they are applied realistically to all manner of concrete situations in school and out of school. Judgments are based on factual evidence. This means the scientific method is related to the humane method. Careful tests prove that this method works.

What has been going forward in Springfield and many other communities is far from perfect. But teachers and school administrators in these communities are reaching not only children at every grade level but they are relating this type of teaching to the work in the churches, the service clubs and all manner of civic groups and organizations.

I refer to Springfield by name not because it has a clearer conception of the human critical faculty, but because in Springfield, as a result of an arrangement made through the National Conference of Christians and Jews this type of teaching has permeated the entire community and has been consistently applied month in and month out, year in and year out. The result is that children and adults are less likely to respond to stimuli which cause blind hatred, hysteria and fear and which appeal to narrow in-group feeling and to personal selfishness.

The Springfield experiment has paralleled and extended similar work in other communities.

What should be taking place now if we are to avoid a postwar world of blind hatreds and hysterias and national and individual selfishness? We should be setting up at once in key communities throughout our nation an educational approach which follows the principles Springfield has absorbed from so many communities—and which, as in Springfield, adapts that approach to conditions peculiar to the individual community.

This is about the only measure that offers any substantial assurance that the fruits of a military victory will not be stolen from us by pro-Fascist and anti-democratic demagogues.

LESSONS FROM THE LEAGUE

By

FELIX MORLEY, Ph.D.

President, Haverford College

In *The Decline of the West,* that profoundly disturbing study in which Oswald Spengler so accurately predicted the advent of totalitarianism, this great German philosopher gave epigrammatic summation to the alleged antithesis between idealism and actuality. This antithesis he regarded as one factor forcing political dictatorship on our demoralized civilization.

"No faith yet has altered the world," asserts Spengler; but conversely, "no fact can ever rebut a faith."

I preface my remarks with this quotation not to provide a text for my observations and still less to indicate that I personally subscribe to all of Spengler's frequently dogmatic reasoning. But from my now distant three-year experience at Geneva, and from my reflections in the twelve years since I left that city, I am profoundly convinced that Spengler is helpful in warning us not to concentrate all our attention on mere mechanisms of international order. And so, while I shall today make a number of criticisms which I believe would be indorsed by most close and objective students of League structure, I want at the outset to emphasize that in the task of building a postwar system, mere architectural perfection is not enough.

The Covenant of the League of Nations had serious defects. They greatly contributed to the failure of that noble experiment and they should be carefully considered and so far as possible eliminated in the establishment of the more effective world organization which I trust is a major objective of this war.

We must always remember, however, that the League of Nations did not fail wholly or even primarily because of its structural and constitutional defects. The League as constituted could have worked successfully if there had been the will, especially in the United States, to make it work. There might well have been no breakdown, and the world would very probably be at peace today, if in 1919 we Americans had shown a fraction of the interest in political success at Geneva that we show today in military success in Tunisia and the Solomon Islands.

Faith alone, to paraphrase Spengler, will not build a viable international order. But neither will the enormous difficulties involved rebut our conviction that this essential step forward can be successfully taken.

If faith and facts are actually irreconcilable then indeed the outlook is as black as Spengler prophesied and the only refuge for the idealist is to endeavor to withdraw, as during the Dark Ages, from a mundane world of sound and fury, signifying nothing. There is, however, at least equal reason for asserting that faith can alter facts, provided the recalcitrance of the latter is given due consideration. Our joint participation in this survey course on "Religion and the World Order" is itself evidence that we agree on the premise that faith can move mountains, Spengler to the contrary notwithstanding.

With realization that faith is both imperative and inadequate, alike for the successful waging of war and the more difficult establishment of peace, we may profitably turn to the specific lessons inherent in the failure of the League of Nations. I do so only after emphasizing that the overriding lesson was our lack of faith in the goal of a balanced and equitable international order.

I hope that now we have that faith which was the Missing Ingredient in 1919. I hope that Americans, to be specific, are now as anxious to see the Four Freedoms apply to Puerto Rico and India as we are to establish them in Slovakia and Poland. Otherwise we are only abandoning isolationism to indorse the opposite and more vicious excess of imperialism. History shows that people less volatile and emotional than ourselves have found it extraordinarily easy to jump from the frying pan into the fire without even being conscious, until too late, of the futility of this transition.

The Covenant of the League of Nations contained four major faults, both implicit and explicit, which cumulatively were certainly in large part responsible for the collapse. It does not follow, as I think I have already adequately suggested, that elimination of these faults would automatically insure a workable international organization. Experience does indicate, however, that attention to the demonstrable defects of the League would greatly improve the chances of success for whatever new structure is reared upon its ruins.

The first of these faults, all of which were general and permeating rather than specific and limited to one or more Articles in the organic act, was psychological. From the beginning the prestige and universal influence of the League was hampered by the fact that the Covenant was made an integral part of a punitive Treaty inflicted by a group of victorious powers on a group of vanquished.

I am not asserting here that the Treaty of Versailles and the satellite settlements imposed upon Austro-Hungary, Bulgaria and Turkey were either undesirably or unjustly rigorous. Indeed, as matters stand today, there is some reason for arguing that Germany was let off too easily in 1918. But that does not alter the unquestionable fact that the Versailles *Diktat,* as it was known in Germany, was precisely that—a dictated peace in which a single nation was forcibly compelled to acknowledge all the blame and responsibility for the war.

Whether or not justifiable, it was a tragic psychological blunder thus to associate the League of Nations, designed to consolidate all nations in building for a brighter future, with the war guilt clause. It meant, unfortunately, that no German citizen could ever work wholeheartedly for the League without thereby opening himself to the charge, which other Germans did not hesitate to make, that he personally repudiated everything for which he and his fellow-countrymen had made heroic sacrifices during more than four years of war. Under the circumstances it is really a tribute to German tolerance that so many of that nation's postwar leaders worked consistently in behalf of an international institution which was legally integrated with a proclamation of their national degradation.

The first lesson to be drawn from League experience, therefore, is that the terms of the postwar settlement and the provisions of the postwar organization for the future preservation of peace should this time be kept wholly distinct and separate. And that will mean that the United States must maintain its present somewhat fervid interest in international cooperation not merely during the emotionalized wartime period, but continuously thereafter, when the inevitable reaction sets in. Then the cry will arise to bring back from distant countries the hundreds of thousands of young Americans whom it is planned to continue in policing tasks during the long Armistice period which must be anticipated. It will be an urgent cry and it will be politically very influential.

As a corollary of this first lesson, of divorce between postwar settlement and postwar reorganization, it should be pointed out that the less punitive the Treaty of Peace the shorter the necessary waiting period before establishment of a promising international organization.

When the war is won, the United Nations, assuming that they remain united, will have to make a difficult choice between punishment of the vanquished and establishment of peace. The more the former is emphasized the longer the latter will have to be postponed. For if we are realistic we shall have to admit that there can be no peace worthy of the name unless the vanquished accept its terms as loyally as the victors. And this acceptance, as we should realize from our common human nature, no people will give sincerely while undergoing a castigation which at least inferentially brands them as inferior. In other words, we can choose between retribution and peace, but we cannot have both simultaneously.

The second general fault inherent in the Covenant of the League of Nations was its emphasis upon the protection and safeguarding of National Sovereignty.

Here again, as in the case of the inclusion of the Covenant in the punitive Treaty of Versailles, it is important to guard against unfair retrospective criticism. The Covenant was included in the Treaty not further to humiliate Germany but primarily because that seemed to President Wilson, Lord Robert Cecil and other League architects the quickest and surest way to get its machinery into actual operation. Similarly the doctrine of national sovereignty was emphasized throughout the League's Constitution primarily because in 1919 any drastic limitation of that doctrine would not have been practical politics.

In spite of the Covenant's complete safeguarding of national authority, as many in this room beside myself are old enough to remember, the League was denounced in this country on the fantastic charge that it was a "Superstate." As such, the critics shouted, it would have power to send American boys to fight in distant places like Armenia. Well, our soldiers are fighting in places more distant than Armenia now. But it was not the authority of the League of Nations —it was rather the lack of any reliable international authority—that sent them there.

Under the League Covenant it was necessary to have the unanimous approval of all member-states as a precedent to almost every action of any consequence. In the words of the first section of Article 5:

> Except where otherwise expressly provided in this Covenant, or by the terms of the present treaty, decisions of any meeting of the Assembly or of the Council shall require the agreement of all the members of the League represented at the meeting.

The vitiating effect of this unanimity rule stands out like a sore thumb in the record of the League of Nations. Its most baneful influence, however, was exerted at the time of the Manchurian crisis, the first step in the unbroken chain of aggression which has led in logical but fatal sequence to the situation in which we find ourselves today. As a permanent member of the Council of the League the Japanese representatives were able to block any action at Geneva under Articles 10 and 11 of the Covenant, both of which required unanimity including the vote of the nation accused of aggression. There would be a parallel for such unanimity if the vote of a jury were forced to include that of the accused whose guilt or innocence is under consideration.

Paragraph 4 of Article 15 of the Covenant does permit a report and recommendations on a dispute by majority vote of the Council. But even here exhaustive preliminaries were necessary and by the time Japan, in the Winter of 1931–32, had skillfully invoked all the delays possible, the occupation of Manchuria was a *fait accompli.* Thus the powerlessness of the League to check aggression on the part of a Great Power was demonstrated—and clearly noted eleven years ago in Rome and Berlin.

Instead of demanding unanimity in all but exceptional cases, the executive organ of postwar government should be authorized to act in behalf of peace by a majority, simple or weighted, in all except clearly specified instances. Only by contracting that area of unrestrained sovereignty which the unanimity rule exemplifies can there be established an international authority worthy of that name.

The second major lesson to be drawn from League experience, therefore, is the necessity of relatively drastic limitations on the doctrine of national sovereignty. Indeed, unless there can be some definite advance over the provisions of the League Covenant in this respect all talk of postwar international organization of a political character is so much wasted breath.

Organization of any kind, from a sand-lot baseball club up, requires some subordination of the will of the individual member to accepted rules. Even my ten year old son realizes that after three strikes he is out—not five strikes for him as against one for the boy to whom he pitches. But nations are in this respect more childish than children. National honor, or unilateral definitions of self-defense, or other pompous shibboleths of sovereignty, simply mean that there shall be no rules of the game except those which the powerful, alone or in alliances, decree shall be established in their own selfish interest.

The point should be labored a little because it takes no prophet to see that this issue of unrestricted sovereignty will be the most difficult of all the problems with which the peacemakers will be confronted.

The paradoxical situation is that we can only fight a modern war, can only support the terrible physical, social and mental strain which it involves, by steadily fanning the flames of patriotism to fever heat. Yet as soon as the war is over, assuming lasting peace to be our objective, this nationalistic psychology must immediately be thrown into reverse.

We must then forthwith emphasize not our own prodigious excellence but the necessity of subordinating ourselves to the welfare of the Community of Nations. And that will mean sacrifice by powerful vested interests and vainglorious politicians as well as by the average citizen of "God's Country." Frankly, I wonder if we can do it. I wonder if, having flexed our muscles and learned our strength we shall be willing to let the three-strike rule apply to us as well as to Wops and Polacks and Chinks and other "lesser breeds without the law"—our law.

In any event, the lesson from the League is clear. All nations, and that includes the U.S.A., must subject themselves to international law. The sovereignty of the United States—let's emphasize that—must be subject to such limitations as international law imposes.

The third major fault of the League of Nations, as I see it, was structural rather than constitutional. It lay in a centralization of policy —a Europeanization of policy one might also say—the more unfortunate because there was no parallel concentration of authority to make concentration of policy rational or effective.

I would sit sometimes in the Council Room at Geneva, listening to that august body discussing the claims of the Hungarian optants, and feel much the same way as I have felt in the press gallery of our Senate when, on District Day, a bill for licensing chiropractors in the city of Washington was reached on the calendar. Why should there not be at least an effort to dispose of local issues through local governmental organs?

It is obvious, however, that no doubts as to the wisdom of making the Council a court of first instance for local issues would assail the representatives of Peru or other non-European nations on the Council. When the Hungarian optants—I shall not stop to tell you who they were—would raise their pathetic voices, all non-European Council members would invariably settle down for a quiet snooze. And all the newspaper men would follow that good example.

The structure of internationalism requires, by definition, a society in the main composed of national units for its basis. And since the mere facts of geography tend to impose a regional layer between the national and the international level of organization it would, I think, be healthy to encourage regional groupings within the universal structure. The chief obstacle to this pattern, in the past, has been the British, and to a somewhat lesser extent the French, Empire, the overseas possessions of which have in both cases been so widely scattered as to make regional organization seem inimical to their far-flung political instincts. Actually there is no conflict, for an empire is itself a special form of regionalism.

It was very apparent at Geneva, in ways other than M. Briand's abortive scheme for European Union, that regionalism is both a natural and a healthy tendency. The Latin-American nations; the Scandinavian states; the Balkan countries and the British Dominions all automatically tended to form blocs in order to present a common front on issues coming before the League. Without those preliminary considerations it is doubtful that the Assembly and its committees could have accomplished anything like as much as was actually achieved at Geneva.

There is a tendency now to picture regionalists and universalists, as the two schools of thought are known, as opposing camps, indorsing rival concepts of eventual world organization. This is unfortunate, for a regional organization like the Pan-American Union and its well-established conferences would assist rather than hamper the work of an overall international organization.

The only stipulation is that the activities of the regional organization should be coordinated with, and should never be hostile or rival to, that of the general association. If that is kept continuously in mind there is no reason why regional associations, including such scattered political groupings as the British Commonwealth of Nations, should be anything but helpful to a restored League. Under such a system many local disputes of an international character could probably be more easily and efficaciously settled by the regional organization, with appeal or reference to the Central Body only when no regional solution can be found.

The third major lesson from League experience is, therefore, that regionalism should be actively encouraged, rather than discouraged, in any new international organization. For the sake of discussion I would personally suggest not one Geneva but five—Geneva itself for a federation of Continental Europe; London for the British Commonwealth of Nations; Moscow for the Soviet Union; Shanghai for an Asiatic Federation; Havana for a Pan-American Union.

The headquarters of the overall organization I would be inclined to place at Ottawa. It should certainly be both outside of Western Europe and away from the capital of any of the most powerful nations. I favor Canada partly because its racial composition makes it a natural catalytic agent for three great peoples—American, British and French; partly because, though quasi-independent, it will never, as a British Dominion, have imperialistic interests of its own; and partly because Canada's geographical location, especially for air travel, makes this American nation a closer neighbor of both Europe and Asia than any other country in the New World.

Aside from the excessive centralization which hampered the functioning of the League of Nations there is another important reason for emphasizing the regional approach in postwar international planning. That approach takes account of political realities. It harmonizes the ideal and the factual considerations in a manner which at least holds hope that we may refute Spengler's gloomy suggestion that faith and facts are irreconcilable.

Two very difficult preliminaries must be accomplished to make an effective world organization even theoretically possible. In the first place, and this is the easier of the two prerequisites, the Axis must be defeated and its own not wholly irrational plans for regional organization, in Europe and Asia, brought to naught. In the second place the Big Three of the United Nations—Great Britain, Russia and the United States—must after victory be willing to subdue their own imperialistic ambitions and their individual concepts of sovereignty in the interest of a collective world order.

Some weeks ago Winston Churchill announced that "we plan to hold our own" and that as long as he is in control no alteration of the structure of the British Empire will be contemplated. More recently, just last week in fact, Secretary Knox advocated that the Japanese-mandated islands in the western Pacific should come not under international but under United States control. Last week, also, the Russian government made it quite clear that Moscow plans to incorporate Estonia, Latvia and Lithuania, still recognized by this country as independent States, into the Soviet Union.[1]

These are only straws in the wind, but they are straws the direction of which Utopians would be well advised to note. Speaking bluntly, I do not myself anticipate that either Great Britain, or Russia, or the United States is likely, in the event of United Nations' victory, to argue strongly for real international control of politically strategic areas. And if that unwilling surmise turns out to be correct it means that regionalism, frankly recognizing the hegemony of a few Great Powers in the areas of their vital interest, is the only approach whereby the universalism attempted at Geneva can eventually be achieved. After all, the problem of securing world order is enormous and any who think it will be attained merely by the wave of an idealistic wand are doomed to bitter disappointment.

There remains one more important lesson from the Geneva breakdown. The new international society, whether or not achieved through regional organization, must make adequate allowances for change and growth. This the League of Nations did not do. It assumed that the political arrangements of the Treaty of Versailles could be maintained unchanged and inviolate, and it assumed this at a time when the stirring of revolutionary forces of tremendous explosive power was already visible beneath the political surface.

A similar mistake must next time be avoided. The new international order must make liberal allowance for the revision of treaties and no unanimity rule, giving blocking power to a single intransigent nation, can be permitted to prevent constant treaty revision in accordance with the judgments of equity and farsighted statesmanship.

Under the policy of "unconditional surrender," to which we are now committed, the initial terms of postwar settlement are almost certain to be in many respects unfair, unwise and impractical. But this need not be fatal if the eventual world organization, representing vanquished as well as victors, is given the authority to revise the immediate settlements and if it is clearly understood that the initial

[1] This lecture was given on February 16, 1943.

punitive arrangements can be altered by procedures other than those of force.

I have noted four major faults—roughly classifiable as psychological, political, structural and organic—which to my mind amply explain why the League of Nations failed. They must be eliminated in whatever new international structure is established after this war. But in closing I want to reiterate what I said at the outset—that the League could have succeeded despite its faults if there had been a universal will to make it work. Conversely, every architectural defect could be remedied and a theoretically perfect international order would similarly fail if the strength of the spirit is again lacking.

Faith and hope in the fraternity of mankind, as opposed to fear and hate between its many racial and religious divisions, must be emphasized simultaneously with the technical planning for a workable international order. Admittedly that will require great tolerance, great forgiveness, great charity, in view of the many incentives to visit upon the aggressors some portion of the suffering they have themselves inflicted.

I do not know whether mankind is big enough for the task, but I do know that unless we mingle the ingredient of faith in the mortar of reconstruction no edifice that we may rear will prove enduring. I do not believe that the exigencies of rhyming alone explain why the poet Tennyson, in "Locksley Hall," unerringly placed the "Parliament of Man"—the meeting of minds in the great human family—ahead of the attainment of World Federation. You know them well, but because they are so apposite I venture to recall a few astonishingly prophetic verses:

"Men, my brothers, men the workers, ever reaping something new:
That which they have done but earnest of the things that they shall do:

"For I dipt into the future, far as human eye could see,
Saw the Vision of the world, and all the wonder that would be;

"Saw the heavens fill with commerce, argosies of magic sails,
Pilots of the purple twilight, dropping down with costly bales;

"Heard the heavens fill with shouting, and there rain'd a ghastly dew
From the nations' airy navies grappling in the central blue;

"Far along the world-wide whisper of the south-wind rushing warm,
With the standards of the peoples plunging thro' the thunder-storm;

"Till the war-drum throbb'd no longer, and the battle-flags were furl'd
In the Parliament of man, the Federation of the world."

SUMMARY

By

F. ERNEST JOHNSON

In reviewing the lectures to which we have listened during these weeks I have reflected first on the title we gave to the course: "Religion and the World Order." Some, no doubt, have questioned at times the aptness of that title. Would we not have been more realistic had we used the formula, "Religion and the World Disorder"? On the whole, I think not. Nothing is more important, it seems to me, in orienting ourselves to the present world situation than to realize that disorder is a kind of order—the wrong kind. For the anarchic situation in the affairs of the world is the product of a prodigious attempt to impose upon men against their wills, and in defiance of an authentic urge in the human spirit, an exploitive order. It is significant that totalitarian claims are put forward under the aspect of "the new order," which the nations are called on to accept and submit to. Tyranny is an "order" which free men abhor, but the only protection we have against it is a valid kind of order. This, I think, these lectures have made clear.

It may be also that some have questioned the applicability of the word religion to some portions of the course. Some of the problems discussed have been stated and analyzed in terms quite as appropriate to a wholly secular setting. But is not this inevitable if religion is conceived as definitely relevant to every aspect of human affairs? The two words, "Religion and" in our title are symbolic of a modern mood with respect to religion, for they denote a nexus between the spiritual and the temporal, the sacred and the "secular." I feel impelled to recall my earlier insistence that identification of religion with the common life of men is the great desideratum of our time—in other words, the overcoming of the secularism of the modern mind.

And here Dr. Tillich's exposition was illuminating and challenging. He has sought to find a resolution of the conflict between a religion that is preoccupied with utopian hopes and one that is drenched with pessimism about man. "Human history," he said, "is neither a mere progress nor a mere tragedy, but it is a fight between the forces of perfection and those of distortion." Succinctly he stated the proposition about which theological controversy now centers: "The belief in Providence . . . gives the certainty that victory over man's existential distortion is won from the point of view of eternity; but it does not give us certainty that there is or will be a victory at any point of history."

This, I think, is a very insightful statement. Between utopianism and social pessimism there is a middle ground. The school of Protestant theologians commonly called "neo-orthodox," in its zeal to deflate the rather superficial optimism that has characterized much of our liberal Christianity, has often seemed to dry up the springs of social hope. If "all prophecy begins with a note of doom" this somber note is not without validity. But a sounder liberalism is, I believe, in the making, one that will avoid the illusions of social perfectionism but will hold to the possibility of progressive realization of moral ideals within history. As Rabbi Bokser said, in his scholarly lecture which merits repeated reading, the God of history transmutes men's cynical laughter into tears, "and those tears into the song of a new redemption."

Reverting now to what was said a moment ago about world order, I stress the point made by Professor Eagleton concerning law and force. The task he outlined was one not of eradicating force—this is sheer romanticism—but rather one of domesticating, as it were, the use of force within a regime of law. Force as a substitute for law is anarchy and brutality; force as a resource for the implementation of law is an indispensable tool of freedom. But the appeal here is to "certain moral principles which can be accepted by all peoples;" without such acceptance there is "no hope for the reconstruction of international law." Here is a charter, in terms of world politics, for the business that you and I have in hand.

Professor Eagleton stressed the centrality of the individual as did

Bishop McConnell. Here again a problem arises in the interpretation of the democratic ideal of life. Against an atomistic conception of society which sets the individual in ultimate isolation from his fellows—standing alone "before God"—Bishop McConnell offered an organic conception, and Rabbi Bokser elaborated the conception in his dissection of dualisms. Man does not exist in a mode of independence and individual moral sovereignty, but always as a member of a community. I covet for the Christian Church in America the sense of corporate being that has always characterized the Jewish community. There is a close and significant relationship between community as experienced in face-to-face relations and world community as we hopefully envisage it today. How shall we achieve that sublimation of sovereignty which Professor MacIver so convincingly contended for in the political realm if we cling to individual sovereignty in the personal realm? Is not the major contribution that religion can make to the realization of democracy, precisely that discipline of the human spirit, wrought in the fellowship of a believing and worshiping community, which makes us "members one of another"? The League of Nations, Dr. Morley told us, had "psychological, political, structural and organic" faults, from all of which the world must learn; but, said he, it "could have succeeded despite its faults if there had been a universal will to make it work." We in America not only lacked such a will, but history, sad to relate, gives evidence of a will to let it fail. The fault here is a moral fault, and political isolationism is a reflection of an inner poverty of the soul. We are strong for democracy so long as it connotes liberty in the sense of freedom from restraints, but for the spiritual discipline that gives meaning to equality, and for the sentiment of fraternity that motivates it we show little enthusiasm. Religion makes its impact on world order in and through a regenerating work upon the individual, making him a glad participant in the corporate experience of community.

It is in this connection that I would like to refer to religious liberty. Dean Weigle presented a considered statement of what he held to be essentials—demands that organized religion may make upon governments. The matter is urgent and the proposals are timely. For my part, I would like to see our several faith groups give at least as much attention to the study of the basis of religious liberty in our own traditions as we give to the formulation of minimal requirements to be presented to the state—and to a world-state if there is to be one.

It is to the credit of modern religion that the problem of religious liberty is so difficult, for the difficulty results from the fact that religion concerns itself more and more with political affairs. Freedom of worship and of religious teaching would be more readily granted if churches and synagogues would contentedly remain "out of politics." But a vigorous Christian or Jewish ethic can accept no such sweeping limitation. Conversely, the minister of religion must realize that public policy is always setting limits to specific kinds of action or of utterance. The price of a broad social religious philosophy is acceptance of many specific restrictions. Concerning such, at any given time, organized religion can demand only equity as between religious groups, and especially for minorities. The boundary between church and state is a moving boundary and religious liberty, like all other liberties, is in large measure a function of the security and stability of the larger community.

Furthermore, it is a corollary of the principle of community which is central in our whole discussion that the effort to win a person to a faith other than his own can never be justified without reference to the cultural ties that bind him. To insist that one may not become a proselyte to a new faith would do violence to religious autonomy. But I am now ready to say that this religious transplantation should never be encouraged except under conditions that make it a free and spontaneous act. Much of the value that has been realized in missionary effort is due to the impact of one religious culture upon another rather than to the religious uprooting of individuals from their cultural soil. I am really contending for a more social conception of religious liberty, one that will see the individual always in some communal setting. Such a conception would set the problem on a new stage, making it less a church-state issue and more an interfaith matter.

This is not to disparage efforts to formulate principles for application to particular situations at particular times. The point is that sweeping generalizations are fallacious and often mischief-making, and the state, however benevolent and enlightened, is not well conceived as a buffer between religious groups. Mr. Frank's presentation of the cultural basis of social order has special significance here. Protestantism, in particular, has been slow to understand the cultural roots of the religious life. This is not to say that any faith group should be barred from approach to a community with which it is culturally unfamiliar. It does mean, however, that in missionary effort the task of cultural orientation is basic. Many missionaries have undertaken this task with much success. The current controversy between Catholics and Protestants over missionary work in Latin America is highly significant and the issues are real. Anything in the nature of a religious monopoly is incongruous. But in their approach to the problem Protestants must not be unmindful of the way in which religion becomes fixed in a cultural pattern.

I should like now to set down some conclusions concerning the significance of the totalitarian threat from the religious point of view.[1] It is because totalitarian systems do something for men which they deeply need that they are so dangerous. If man is forlorn without any gods he is in a perilous state when he surrenders himself to half-gods. Psychiatrists recognize the possibility, in seeking a valid integration of an individual's life, of effecting a spurious integration—an organization of the self on an inadequate plane. So with peoples; when there is no vision of a Most High, they shape base images and echo the ancient cry: "These be thy gods, O Israel!" Nazism is a religion which creates community and frees the individual from the futility and ineptitude that result from purposeless isolation. But the cup that community drinks of is a poison cup, and its last state is worse than its first.

All this is perhaps elementary. But the inference to be drawn is not so obvious. I am definitely suggesting that Western democracy has failed —partly because religion has failed—to create a community in the spiritual sense that will do for the individual on a plane of nobility and universality what, lacking such achievement, he is bound to seek on a lower level. This acceptance for our democratic countries and our churches and synagogues of a measure of guilt for the present world tragedy has no relevance to the urgency and necessity of winning the

[1] The course included an instructive lecture on this subject by Dr. Hans Simons of the New School for Social Research, which is not available for publication.

war, but it has a mighty relevance to the establishment of a durable world order. We who stand in the Judaic-Christian tradition are custodians of a high humanistic faith—in the sense apprehended by Bishop McConnell, grounded in ethical monotheism. It is our task to infuse into democracy a spiritual dynamic which will make it more than a political concept, which will make it veritably a universal way of life.

Nazism is not only particularistic, anti-universal, but opportunistic, unstable, unpredictable. Many persons have seen here a disturbing parallel to extreme pragmatism as expounded by some of our own philosophers. In their eagerness to achieve wholeness, adequacy and security within man's life they seem to overlook the necessity to see all life "under the aspect of eternity." It is here, I may remark parenthetically, that I would question the adequacy of a part of Mr. Frank's very able analysis.

Every listener must have responded inwardly with sympathy to Father LaFarge's characterization of the grist of reconstruction proposals which is piling up around our intellectual mills. "They are devoted," he said, "to saving all that is possible of the old world, for fear of a much worse state of things if we depart from the sound lessons of the past. Or they are for sweeping revolutions, taking the opportunity now or never to rebuild the world according to their desire." I was much interested in Father LaFarge's proposal that religion undertake to buttress itself against atheistic assaults by repeated and positive affirmations of the centrality of religion and the existence of God. This is a wholesomely frank appeal for "indoctrination" at a time when it has fallen into disrepute in a large part of the educational world. It would probably be well for educators to be less supercilious about indoctrination since most of us, consciously or unconsciously, do a good deal of it! It should be noted that Father LaFarge, in his subsequent comments, abated nothing of the Thomist's insistence on the exaltation of reason. His appeal to the efficacy of simple, forceful affirmation has much foundation in experimental psychology. Here Dr. Miller's very interesting exposition of the methods of propaganda is pointedly relevant. Propaganda, he insists, may be quite justifiable if it is honest. Personally, I question the efficacy of *mere* doctrinal affirmations except as they are media for a heritage of faith which is kept open to rational validation, to the extent that reason can operate with reference to them. Faith, after all, is different from knowledge; if that were not true we should not need the word faith at all. It has an active and voluntary quality that defies coercion, even of a mental sort.

As for the uses of propaganda, I wish we might have some criteria of internal validity in terms of *method,* independently of the substantive valuation to be placed on the ends sought. Surely opinion making as a process should be subject to some appraisal without reference to whether the opinion itself is sound or not. I am thinking particularly of such common faults as giving the reader, listener or spectator a part of the known relevant facts under pretense of giving him all he requires for an honest judgment; juggling statistics; in a word, using any of the devices Dr. Miller listed in a way that involves deliberate deception. We cannot "analyze" propaganda without some definite notion of what constitutes illegitimate propaganda.

I shall take time to single out only one point for comment in Dr. Van Dusen's clear analysis of reconstruction proposals. He reminded us that almost all the plans that have been offered for rebuilding the political structure of the world make one common assumption: that power is the dominant factor in world order and can no longer be by-passed. Are we equal to the task of integrating moral idealism with political realism? It is a fundamental error to seek a solution of the problem of power by avoiding its exercise. Here again we are reminded of Dr. Eagleton's insistence that force must be regularized, and thus socialized, under law.

To my mind the economic base of political order is of primary importance. At this point experience under the Versailles Treaty and the League is instructive—though it would be a grievous error to suppose that preoccupation with economic at the expense of political factors would lead to happier results. Unless an economic base for substantial security is laid in every nation, there can be no adequate degree of political stability. And what I call Economic Problem Number One now to be solved is the achievement of substantially full employment through the conquest of the business cycle. Dr. Buell made an illuminating analysis of this problem, pointing out what he conceived to be the dangers from the "right" and from the "left." In my own view we are approaching a mixed economy in which public and private enterprise will be interrelated.

For us in this group the ethical issue of the profit motive here comes to the fore. May I repeat some comments that I have made previously on this subject: "On Christian assumptions, ethics cannot be excluded from economics. The individual always has the option between a short-range and a long-range view of his responsibilities, and the difference between them is often the difference between immediate, private economic advantage and a sound economic policy for society as a whole.

"Moreover, the merits of the profit system and the validity of the profit motive are different issues. Profit, in the strict sense of the word, is a form of gain that is independent of actual service rendered, since that is compensated by salaries, wages and bonuses. The classical economists divided the product of industry into four parts: wages of labor, including salaries; interest on capital at some definite 'going' rate; rent on land, determined by its 'marginal' value; and profit, which is all that is left, and belongs to the 'enterpriser'. The first three are relatively 'fixed' by the market; the last has no limit. It may of course be negative, that is, loss. By the same token it may be 1,000 per cent gain. The classical theory required this indeterminate category as a motivator of enterprise. The question to what extent it is necessary is a factual question in psychology, to be answered by experimentation. It becomes a theological question, too, inasmuch as current theological controversy centers about the nature of man and his capacity for high moral action. But here again the issue is whether and to what extent men will do their best work as economic enterprisers without the prospect of *speculative* gain."

The implication for the domestic problem of full employment of the foreign trade situation should be clear. We are now in imminent danger of reversing a wholesome policy implemented by the reciprocal trade treaties, and thus impeding both the achievement of domestic economic stability and the development of international good will.[2]

Seldom have I heard so carefully balanced, and yet courageously liberal, a presentation of the labor problem as that of Dr. Fitch. The

[2] See footnote on page 111.

essential point, so often missed, is that the legislative and the administrative policies developed in recent years with reference to labor in America have been aimed at establishing a reasonable degree of equality of status between industrial labor on the one hand and ownership and management on the other. Until that could be achieved, no attempt at an even-handed, impartial policy on the part of government would have been possible. As Dr. Fitch frankly said, we now have to look to organized labor to develop an internal discipline commensurate with improvement of status. The changed situation calls for a different strategy with reference to labor on the part of church and synagogue.

Who is wise enough to foresee the developments in the years just ahead in the field of government, of which Dr. Brunner in thorough and expert fashion gave us the background? Are we approaching a new era in the government of democratic nations? May it be that the traditional American idea that the best government is the one that governs least is passing into eclipse, and that a welfare theory of government is emerging? For my part, I welcome every sign that the old notion of the state as a necessary evil—an encroaching power to be forever guarded against—is passing. To many this means the advent of totalitarianism, or at least of authoritarianism in government. It need not be so. Political Problem Number One is the perfection of governmental procedures which match the increased tempo of social change and which can tame a gargantua of technology while at the same time maximizing liberty through the self-government of a disciplined people.

And now, finally, the role of education in the postwar world, insightfully delineated for us by Dr. Counts, claims our attention. Dr. Counts pointed out the startling fact, documented both in the annals of the Soviet Union and in the recent history of Germany, that education can change the temper and outlook of a whole people. Education is no longer to be considered the function of the schools alone. It is a total community enterprise. The entire pattern of our life educates more fundamentally than any formal schooling. And whence comes the grand conception of life of which Dr. Counts speaks? For you and me the heritage of the Judaic-Christian tradition is a primary source and entails a special responsibility. Three things, said Dr. Counts, come to us from that source—belief in the worth of persons, the concept of the universal brotherhood, and the quality of mercy. These are resources which we must draw upon for the reeducation of our people with reference to the relations of races and cultures as well as of individuals. Within such a framework we should be able to translate technology from mechanism into redemptive enterprise. In the name of those great affirmations of our common faith we must find a solvent for the racial and class conflicts that hang over our democratic experiment like the sword of Damocles.

INDEX

Accident compensation, 157
Adult education, 132
Advertisements, American, 187-188
Agricultural Adjustment Acts, 174-175
Ahab, 45
America, grand conception of, 135
American dream, 176-178
American Institute of Judaism, 144
American point of view, 60-65
American Society of International Law, 139
American system, 103
Amery, Mr., 67
Anarchism, 79
Anglo-American cooperation, 109-110
Anglo-Saxon democracy, 27
Anti-Christian ideology, 31
Anti-Jewish ideology, 31
Antisemitism, in early Germany, 131
Anxiety, 23
Archbishop of Canterbury, 33, 87-88
Argentina beef, 110
Atheism, 77
  in Russia, 31
Atlantic Charter, 81, 139
Augustine, 47
Australia, social security in, 173, 175
Automobile Workers Union, C.I.O., 163

Baal, 45
Babel, Tower of, 23-24
"Back to normalcy," 153
"Band Wagon" device, 180
Barth, Karl, 24, 86
Bases of a Just and Durable Peace, Study Conference on, 32-33
Beard, Charles A., 136
Beveridge, Sir William, 154, 165
Beveridge Report, 110
Bill of Rights, 36, 156
Bismarck, 173
Bodin, 95
Bokser, Ben Zion, 77-92, 208, 209
Bourgeois humanism, 20
Bourgeois society, modern, 21
Briand, M., 202
British Commonwealth of Nations, 202
British Empire, 61-62
British point of view, 60-65
British Weekly, 86
Brother Lawrence, 6
Browder, Earl, 83
Brunner, Edmund De S., 167-178, 215
Buchman, Frank, 186
Buell, Raymond Leslie, 101-112, 213
Bury, J. B., 29

Canterbury, Archbishop of, 33, 87-88
Capitalists, 81-82
"Card Stacking" device, 180
Catholic Church, and international law, 144
Catholicism, 25-26, 27
CCC camps, 132, 169, 172
Cecil, Robert, Lord, 30, 198
Children:
  exploitation of, 134
  in Western culture, 125-127
China:
  Christian movement in, 31
  postwar, 57
Christian and the War, The, 87
Christian Century, 85, 86, 87
Christian church, and segregation of Jews, 184-185
Christian Church and World Order, The, 33
Christian Front, 186

Christianity:
as a Jewish sect, 8
value put on individuals by, 44-45, 46
Christianity and Crisis, 80, 89
Church:
and state, separation of, 36-37
and world, 9
religious freedom of, 35-36
unity of, 26
Churchill, Winston, 203
Citizens, religious freedom of, 36
City of God, 47
Civil rights, and workers, 156
Class consciousness, 48-49
Coffin, Henry Sloane, 89
Collective bargaining, 158
Colonies, 55
Commandments, 125
Commission of the Churches for International Friendship and Social Responsibility, British, 33
Commission to Study the Organization of Peace, 145
Common Ground, 88
Common man, 58
Communism, 77, 81-85
as "poison" word, 185, 186, 189, 190
Communist, The, 82, 83
Communists:
in America, 83
understanding of education, 134-135
Community, value of, 97
Conditioned reflex, 180
Confederation, 59
Conferences, pronouncements on religious liberty, 32
Congregation, religious freedom of, 35-36
Constitution, 59
religious freedom in, 31-32
Constitutional change, 96-97
Constitutional Limitations, 32
Cooley, Justice, 32
Copernicus, 124
Corporate worship, 7
Corpus Christi, 8
Corpus Christianum, 8
Coughlin, Father, 186, 189, 190
Counts, George S., 131-137, 215-216
Covenant of the League of Nations, 30
Craft unions, 107
Crime, 164
Cripps, Sir Stafford, 67
Cultural basis of postwar reconstruction, 113-130
Culture, 116
definition of, 118
Western European, 122-129
Current Religious Thought, 77

Daily Worker, The, 84
Dark Ages, Christianity in, 47
Davies, D. R., 86
Declaration of Independence, 11, 73
Decline of the West, The, 195
Defeatist viewpoint, 128
Deism, 20
Democracy, 27, 50, 91
conceptions of, 51-52
definitions of, 39-40
English and American, 40, 109-110
religion and, 39-52
Democratic ideal, 11
Depression, great, 170-171
Despair, 23
Deuteronomy, 46
Dewey, John, 6
Dialectical Religious Socialism, 22, 25, 27-28
Dies, Martin, 186-187
Divine Providence, 22, 23
Drucker, Peter, 134
Dualism, 85-89
Dynamics of Industrial Democracy, The, 158

Eagleton, Clyde, 139-151, 208, 213
Easton, W. Burnett, 87
"Economic royalist," 185
Ecumenical Protestantism, 25, 26-27
Education:
for worker, 155
free, 156
in postwar world, 131-137
pre-school, 132
secularization of, 12-16
Elijah, 45

Empire, 202
Employment, 101-102
Engels, quoted, 82
England, social security in, 173
Enlightenment, 20, 22
Erasmus, 20
European Union, 202
Evil, 78
Ezekiel, 47

Fair Labor Standards Act, 156
Faith, 195, 196
Far East, New Order of, 55
Farm Security Administration, 172
Fascist propaganda, 190
Fascist totalitarianism, 26
Federal Council of the Churches of Christ in America, 34, 144
Federalism, 59
Federal Security Agency, 169, 172
Federal Trade Commission, 174
First World War, 29, 80, 81
Fitch, John A., 153-165, 214, 215
Force, use of, 141
Fortune, 101, 171
Four Freedoms, 196
Four Great Powers of United Nations, 60
Frank, Lawrence K., 113-130, 211, 212
Frankfurter, Justice, 156, 159
Free World, 130
French people, 67
Freud, 22
Future of Industrial Man, The, 134

Galileo, 124
Generalities, 179
Geneva, 202-203
Geopolitics, 133
German people, 58
  and Nazis, 80
Germany, 79, 80, 91
  future of, 54
  social security in, 173
Gibbon, Edward, 42
Gillis, James M., 77
Gladstone, 41
Golden, Clinton, 158, 162
Government, emerging role of, 167-178
Grand Coulee dam, 174
Great Britain, church in, 31
Greek Orthodox churches, 27
Grotius, 140

Havana, 203
Hearst, William Randolph, 186, 190
Hegel, 20
Heimann, Eduard, 80, 81
Herald Tribune Forum, 81
History of Freedom of Thought, 29
Hitler, 79, 83, 87
  as propagandist, 185-188
Hoover, Herbert, 83, 168, 170
Hopkins, Ernest Martin, 81
Hull Trade Agreements Act, 111
Human beings, value put on, 44-45, 46
Human Destiny, 86
Humanism, 43-44, 48, 51
Humanist, 47

Iceberg Patrol, 150
Ideological revolution, 167-168
Imperialism, 55, 63
Imports, 109-110
India, liberation of, 63
Individual, religious freedom of, 34-35
Industrial Revolution, 167
Inter-American Juridical Committee, 140, 145
International Friendship and Social Responsibility, Commission of the churches for, 33
International government, 151
International law, 201
  past failure of, 140-151
  reconstruction in, 139-151
  responsibility for, in democracy, 143
International Missionary Council, 34
International power, postwar, 54
Interstate Commerce Commission, 169-170
Isolationism, national, 79, 96

Japan, 57, 79, 80, 91
  and League of Nations, 199-200
Japanese, 58
  understanding of education, 134

Jefferson, Thomas, 73, 159
Jeremiah, 47
Jesus, 24, 46
"Jew," 184-185
Jewish people, 29, 37
  as scapegoats, 90
Jezebel, 45
Johnson, F. Ernest, 3-16, 207-216
Judaic-Christian tradition, 8, 135
Judaism:
  Reform, 88
  value put on individuals by, 44-45, 46
Justice, world, 91

Kairos, 28
Kant, 41
Kelly, Fred C., 181
Kepler, 124
Kierkegaard, 23
Kingdom of God, 22, 24
Knox, Secretary, 203
Kook, Abraham Isaac, 91-92
Ku Klux Klan, 186

Labor, in postwar world, 153-165
Labor policy, 106-108
Labor racketeering, 106
Labor unions:
  lack of democratic procedure in, 163
  numbers in, 161
La Farge, John, 67-75, 212
Laissez faire, 7, 105, 168
Latin-American countries, church in, 31
Lawrence, Brother, 6
Lazaron, Morris S., 88
League of Nations, 30, 56, 59, 142, 150
  an American device, 62, 63
  Covenant of, 195, 197-200
  lessons from, 195-206
Lehman, Herbert, 72-75
Lenin, V. I., 82, 84
Leviticus, 46
Liberty, personal, 96
Lincoln, Abraham, 40, 41-42
Living standards, improved, 102
Living wage, 154-155
"Locksley Hall," 205-206
Lodge, Henry Cabot, 57, 146
Loew, Judah, 90
London, 203
Luther, Martin, 20, 47
Lutherans, 27

MacIver, Robert M., 93-100
Maimonides, 80
Management, paternalistic, 162
Manchurian crisis, 199-200
Mann, Horace, 12, 13
Manpower Commission, 169
Marshall, Chief Justice, 150
Marx, Karl, 50, 82
Marxism, 22, 28, 81-85, 90
  anti-religious propaganda of, 84-85
McConnell, Francis J., 39-52, 209, 212
Mead, Margaret, 118
Mediaeval synthesis, 7, 10
Medicine, advance in, 128
Meiklejohn, Alexander, 159
Melancholy, 23
Methodist Church, 47
Micah, 78
Middle Ages, church in, 9, 18
Militarist Christians, 87
Mill, John Stuart, 168, 171
Miller, Clyde R., 179-193, 212, 213
Minorities, 30-31, 144
  freedom for, 102
Missionary Council, International, 34
Modern Era, 56
Moneyed class, 48
Moralistic theism, 20
Moral Rearmament, 186
Morley, Felix, 195-206, 209
Morrison, Charles Clayton, 87
Mosaic laws, 41
Moscow, 203
"Muddling through," 61
Multiplicity, 99
Mysticism, 42-43

Naboth, 45
Name calling, 179, 184
Nash, Arnold, 84
National Association of Manufacturers, 103

National Conference of Christians and Jews, 193
National Labor Relations Act, 157, 164, 176
National Resources Planning Board, 109
Naturalistic pessimism, 22-25
Nazis, 79, 131
  understanding of education, 134
Nazism, 24, 77
Nazi-Soviet Pact, 83
Negroes, 191, 192
  and labor unions, 160, 162
  and the vote, 156
  segregation of, 184
Netherlands, church in, 31
New Deal, 64, 83, 103
  international, 55, 56
New England, Puritan, 10
New Order, 57
  international, 64
  of Far East, 55
New Republic, The, 159
New Testament, 46
Newton, 124
New World Order, Statement of American Proposals for, 34-35
New Zealand, social security in, 173
Niebuhr, Reinhold, 85, 86
Nietzsche, 22
Nordic race, 79
Norway, church in, 31
NYA, 132, 172

Oath, respect for, 123-124
Old Testament prophets, 8
On to Orthodoxy, 86
OPA, 105
Opinion-making, in postwar world, 179-193
Ottawa, 203
Oxford Conference, 27
Oxford Movement, 186

Pacifism, 21, 86
Paddock, Bishop, 191
Pagan ideology, 31
Palestine, 88, 91
Pan-American Union, 202
Parker, Theodore, 40
Parliamentarism, 82
Pavlov, 180
Pax Britannica, 56
Peace Conference, 30
Pegler, Westbrook, 186, 190
Personality disintegration, 124
Personal liberty, 96
Pessimism, 86
  naturalistic, 22-25
"Plain folks" device, 180
Plant, Dr., 125
"Poison" words, 184
Police force, 54
Political revolution, 167
Pope Pius XII, 144
Postwar reconstruction:
  Catholic view, 67-75
  Jewish view, 77-92
  proposals for, 53-65
  Protestant view, 53-65
  responsibility for, 60
Postwar world:
  education in, 131-137
  labor in, 153-165
  non-school agencies in, 133
  opinion-making in, 179-193
  religious liberty in, 29-37
Presbyterian Churches of Great Britain and Ireland, Conference of, 32
Pre-school education, 132
Prince, Mr., 103
Private industry, 108
Propagandists, devices used by, 179-181
Prophets, Old Testament, 8
Psalms, 80
Public Health Service, 168-169, 170
Puritan New England, 10

Racial superiority, 160
Racketeering, union, 163
Real politik, 56
Reconstruction, postwar, 53-65 (*see also* Postwar reconstruction):
  cultural basis of, 113-130
  economic basis of, 101-112
  in international law, 139-151
  political basis of, 93-100

Reeducation, 31
Reformation, 7, 47, 80
Reform Judaism, 88
Regional groupings, 201-202
Regionalism, 202
Rehabilitation in liberated countries, 72-75
Religion, 84
Religion:
  and democracy, 39-52
  and science, 123
  as phase of culture, 5
  definition of, 18
  in building postwar world, 68
  warfare against, 72
Religious classics, study of, 15
Religious liberty:
  in postwar world, 29-37
  rights included in, 34-36
Religious Socialism, 22, 27-28
Religious thought:
  trends in, 17-28
  types of, 19
Republican Party, 57, 111
Revolution, 24, 59, 167-168
Rickenbacker, Eddie, 190
"Right to work," 155, 157
Ritschl, 20
Roman Catholicism, 25-26, 31, 37
Roman Empire, 8, 42
Roosevelt, F. D., 83
"Rosy Glow" words, 179, 184, 187
Russian people, 131
Ruttenberg, Harold, 158, 162

Scandinavia, social security in, 173
Scapegoat, 90
Schleiermacher, Friedrich, 20
Schooner Exchange case, 150
Schuman, Fredrick L., 85
Science, 10
  and religion, 123
Scientific Monthly, 123
"Secular," meaning of, 3
Secularism, 4
  contemporary, 3-16
Secularization of education, 12-16
Securities Exchange Commission, 174
Security, in Roosevelt administrations, 172
Shanghai, 203
Sherman Act, 174
Shotwell, James T., 33
Simons, Hans, 211
Sin, 78
Slavery, 47
Smith, Adam, 168, 171
Smith, Gerald L. K., 186
Social cohesion of Jews, 46-47
Social contacts, 43
Social creeds, 4
Social disorder, 124
Social Gospel, 4, 20
Socialism, early religious, 22, 27-28
Socialist dictatorship, 105
Social outlook, effect of religious thought on, 17-28
Social security, 157-158
Social Security Board, 172
Society, Christian, 8
Soul, Christian teaching concerning, 44
Sovereignty, 94-96
Soviet Union, 131
Spengler, Oswald, 195, 196, 203
Spofford, William B., 191
Springfield, Mass., 192-193
State, church and, separation of, 36-37
Subject peoples, 55
Subsidies, government, 104

Tariffs, high, 104
Taxation, 106
Teachings of Karl Marx, The, 82
Tennyson, Alfred, Lord, 205
Testimonial device, 179, 185
Theological humanism, 20
Threshold, 85
Tillich, Paul J., 17-28, 208
"Tory," 185
Totalitarian state, 29, 31, 97
Tower of Babel, 23-24
Toynbee, Arnold, 42, 108-109
Trade agreements, 158
Trade names, 187
Transfer device, 179, 185
Treaty, 141
Trial and error, 61

Tribalism, 79
TVA, 174

Unions, 106-108
United Nations, 30, 31, 139, 179, 198
  Big Three of, 203
  Four Great Powers of, 60
United States, church in, 31
Unity of Church, 26
Universalists, 202
Universal Postal Union, 150
Utopians, 56, 204

Van Dusen, Henry P., 53-65, 213
Vansittart, Sir Robert, 57
Vatican, concordat with Hitler, Franco, 185
Versailles treaty, 56, 59, 62, 197
Victorian age, liberalism in, 48-49
Violence, law as restraint of, 141
Voluntary associations, 48, 49

War, modern, 147-150
Weigle, Luther A., 29-37, 209
Western European culture, 122-129
Wilhemina, Queen, 81
Willkie, Wendell, 57
  world tour of, 67
Wilson, Woodrow, 30, 198
Winrod, Gerald, 189
World:
  church and, 9
  grand conception of, 136
World community, 133
World Government, 58
World justice, 91
World Society, postwar, 55, 58
World War I, 103
Worship, corporate, 7
WPA, 169, 172

Lightning Source UK Ltd.
Milton Keynes UK
UKOW052317180712

196238UK00001B/117/A

9 781406 748963